NOT EVEN PAST

NOT EVEN PAST

A HISTORY OF THE
DEPARTMENT OF ENGLISH,
THE OHIO STATE UNIVERSITY,
1870–2000

Morris Beja

AND

Christian Zacher

IMPROMPTU PRESS

COLUMBUS

Library of Congress Cataloging-in-Publication Data is available online at catalog.loc.gov.

Cover design by Mary Ann Smith
Text design by Juliet Williams
Type set in Adobe Minion Pro

To our colleagues and students, over the years

The past is never dead. It's not even past.

—Gavin Stevens, in
William Faulkner, *Requiem for a Nun*

CONTENTS

ILLUSTRATIONS

PREFACE

WE HOPE this volume provides what literary historians call a "usable past." We believe that whatever uses, or lessons, can be derived from it apply not only to the Department of English at Ohio State, and in fact not only to other English Departments, but across many disciplines at many colleges and universities.

From the beginning, our plan has been to concentrate on the twentieth century. We do have a chapter on "The Early Years," and at the end an Epilogue ("Into the Twenty-First Century"). After that first chapter, we have one on Joseph Denney and then on the tenure of each Chair after that. Within each chapter, we try to proceed chronologically, as programs and important faculty appointments come along, but we occasionally violate strict chronology. We recognize that that is not the only way we could have structured the book, but it seemed to us the most logical way.

We have tried to be honest and fair in discussing various controversies and disputes, but we can't pretend to be totally objective or impartial. Certainly, we have not provided a whitewash that ignores problems the Department has had over the years. But we're also confident that our respect, admiration, and very often our affection for the Department, and for our colleagues and students, are never in doubt.

CHAPTER 1

Our Mother Tongue

The Early Years

AT FIRST it was touch and go. The very first resolution at the very first meeting (May 11, 1870) of the Board of Trustees of the Ohio Agricultural and Mechanical College—what was to be called The Ohio State University in 1878—stated that the course of study of the College "should be only that pertaining to agriculture, stock and the mechanic arts; or any thing pertaining to their progress and development." Supporting that view, one member of the Board of Trustees—Norton S. Townshend, who was also the president of the State Board of Agriculture—asserted that the College "should educate our farmers as farmers, and mechanics as mechanics." In contrast, another member, T. C. Jones, claimed that the aim "was not to teach boys to plow, but to educate them."[1]

When the issue was revisited on January 6 of the next year, a small committee of five members recommended that a wide group of disciplines be covered within the College, including "English language and literature" and "modern and ancient languages." "The report was adopted, only one member

---

1. *The First Annual Report of the Board of Trustees of the Ohio Agricultural and Mechanical College* (1872), 42. Subsequent citations will be to "*Second Annual Report,*" etc. As Professor David Frantz has remarked in a note to the authors, a sign of how the "the power of the College of Agriculture remained legendary into the early 1980s" is the perhaps apocryphal story that the "long-time Dean of the College (and later named Vice President for Agricultural Affairs) Roy Kottman, when asked if he would consider running for governor of the state of Ohio quipped that he would never 'step down' to such a position."

voting against it."[2] But when the Board voted to establish ten departments of instruction, including one of "English and modern and ancient languages," the vote was eight to seven. As James E. Pollard noted in his history of Ohio State, "it was this margin of a single vote which cast the die forever on the right side of the balance."[3]

When, in consequence of that decision, ten original professorships were created, the first to be listed, not surprisingly, was in "Agriculture," the second and third in "Physics and Mechanics" and in "Mathematics and Civil Engineering." Eighth came "English language in its higher departments, with such instruction in our mother tongue as will give our pupils easy and exact expression of their thoughts or discoveries, and enable them to communicate them to others in a clear and intelligible manner." The ninth and tenth professorships were in "Ancient Languages—that is, Latin and Greek," and "Political Economy and Civil Polity." "English" was a bit of a misnomer, for "To this chair will be added the modern languages, by which is intended the French and German—to open to our students the rich stores of agricultural and scientific knowledge to be found therein."[4]

So the first head of the "English" department, Joseph Millikin, taught German (two courses) and French, as well as English, all, he said, "more than I can do with perfect justice to myself or the branches I teach."[5] The course in English was intensely philological; it included required readings in Francis A. March, *Introduction to Anglo-Saxon: An Anglo-Saxon Reader* and John Earle, *The Philology of the English Tongue,* as well as *The Vision of Piers Ploughman,* "critically read"; "Chaucer critically read"; and George L. Craik's *The English of Shakespeare.* Incidentally, "The requirements of admission to any of these courses are a good common school education, including the elements of Algebra."[6]

Millikin was a former preacher, but, according to a reminiscence by T. C. Mendenhall, the College's first professor of Physics and Mechanics,

> having a philosophical and critical mind his preaching became less and less satisfactory to his congregations, mostly rural, who adhered strictly to the orthodox standards of the time, and about 1870 he abandoned the idea of entering the ministry, accepting, in 1871, the professorship of Greek language in Miami University. From Miami he came to Columbus to fill the chair of

2. *First Annual Report,* 71.
3. Pollard, *History of The Ohio State University,* 17.
4. *Second Annual Report,* 5.
5. *Fourth Annual Report,* 680.
6. *Third Annual Report,* 48–49.

FIGURE 1.1. Joseph Millikin

English and Modern Languages and Literature, in which he sat more at ease than in that of Ancient tongues.[7]

No doubt justifiably feeling overworked, Millikin lobbied, unsuccessfully, that his position be divided in two, into English and the Modern Languages.[8] Instead, the Board appointed Alice K. Williams as an "assistant" in the Department.

Williams thus became the first female member of the faculty, and for a short time the Department faculty was half female—although in fact she taught French and German. (The College then had nineteen women among its ninety-nine students.)[9] But when Professor Albert H. Tuttle "moved that Miss Williams be invited to take a seat with the faculty," Mendenhall moved that the motion be tabled.[10]

---

7. *The First Faculty,* quoted in Dasher, *A Brief History,* 3.
8. *Fourth Annual Report,* 680.
9. Pollard, *History of the Ohio State University,* 37.
10. "Faculty Minutes, 14 September 1877," University Archives. The story was also reported to us as family lore by Claire Cooper, not herself a relative. Williams was the great aunt of

FIGURE 1.2. Alice Williams

In 1875, two years after the University actually began offering classes, Millikin—by then having been given the additional appointment of Librarian for the College—also had to complain of a lack of texts, noting that

> to teach English, French, and German philology, with not a text of the earlier or middle period (save the one read in the class-room) accessible to the student, is like teaching geology without a fossil, or surveying without a compass. . . . Like others of the Faculty, I gladly loan books of my own not needed for daily reference, but such loans are expensive and inconvenient to the teacher, and wholly inadequate for a class's needs. I therefore earnestly recommend an appropriation for the purchase of at least the following works:

> *Turner*—History of the Anglo-Saxons.
> *Freeman*—History of the Norman Conquest.

---

another early woman faculty member, Gertrude Lucille Robinson (Instructor, 1916–19; B.A., 1913; M.A., 1916). Cooper's godmother, "Aunt Monie," was Robinson's sister. Williams left Ohio State in 1889 and returned to her home town, Urbana, Ohio; she died there in 1925.

Morris—Edition of Chaucer.

Dyce—Edition of Shakespeare.

Morris and Skeat—Specimens of Early English.

Wackernagel—Deutsches Lesebuch.

Wackernagel—Alt-franzosiches Lesebuch.

Littre—Dictionnaire Français.

Brachet—Dictionnaire Etymologique.

Skeat—Edition of Marlowe.

Morris—Edition of Spenser.[11]

By 1876, as Nancy Dasher observes in her history of the Department, the *Sixth Annual Report* describes "what we would now call a Major in English."[12] Well, maybe not "now":

> The elective course in the school of English . . . is designed to help the student, first, to a philological knowledge of his mother tongue, its resources, both grammatical and lexical, and its relationships to other languages; second, to the intelligent and sympathetic study of English literature of the various periods; and third, to the acquirement of such linguistic, rhetorical, and logical principles and habits as shall enable him to put good thinking into good English, written and oral. . . .
>
> And certainly the attainment of the first includes and necessitates the study of Anglo-Saxon.

This section of the report, signed by Millikin, supports those assertions by quoting, for example, the philologist Hiram Corson's declaration that the student "who would grow up to the fullest appreciation and enjoyment of the great masterpieces of English literature must seek out the ancient mother"—that is, the ancient mother tongue.[13]

By 1879, Millikin was being assisted by Assistant Professor of History and Philosophy, John T. Short, who became head of the Department of History and English Language and Literature when Millikin resigned and French and German became a separate department in 1881. Short died soon after having to resign because of ill health; the Trustees' report of 1883 states that the "vacancy caused by his resignation has been filled by the election of Miss Cynthia U. Weld, A. M., Professor of Rhetoric and History in the Ohio University. Her rank is that of assistant professor." Weld thus became the first woman to

---

11. *Fifth Annual Report,* 54.
12. Dasher, *A Brief History,* 6.
13. *Sixth Annual Report,* 77–78.

head the Department—and the last for over a century. She was, in fact, the first woman to head any department in the University. Her selection was not unanimous: the vote was four to one; James H. Anderson voted no.[14]

Her tenure in charge didn't last long. In 1885 the Board appointed a committee "to correspond with the leading universities of the country with a view to securing men of high character and attainments who were available and eligible to the vacancies in the faculty. The same committee was also directed to secure and recommend to the trustees for election a professor of history and English language and literature." The Board then duly voted to appoint George W. Knight, of the University of Michigan, to that position.[15]

Knight—who would serve the University for over four decades—came to feel that his position was less that of a "Chair" than of a "settee," since, as Pollard puts it, "it also covered political science, economics and sociology as far as they went in those days."[16] Nevertheless, by 1887 "the department of history and English language and literature, which has been under the very able direction of Professor Knight, assisted by Mr. A. H. Welsh, has been divided, Professor Knight being placed in charge of the chair of history and political science, and Mr. Welsh in charge of the department of English language and literature as assistant professor."[17] In that year, a Bachelor of Arts degree was awarded to Joseph Russell Taylor—destined to be known in subsequent years as a prominent member of the faculty of the English Department and as one of "Denney's boys." Welch died in 1891, succeeded briefly by James A. Chalmers of Eureka College, and then in 1893 by A. C. Barrows, of the Agricultural College at Ames, Iowa.

In 1891 the *Lantern* published a detailed profile of the Department, which claimed that "There is no condition of life, no religious aspiration, no complication of human motives and emotions, no ethical relation, which literature does not illume." According to the article, students in the first year studied David J. Hill's *Elements of Rhetoric and Composition: A Text-book for Schools and Colleges*. In the second year "subjects for written exercises" included works by Shakespeare, Coleridge, Longfellow, Macaulay, Addison, Scott, Daniel Webster, George Eliot, and Hawthorne. The history of the English language was concentrated on through Chaucer, with a stress on memorization ("The Prologue and Knight's Tale are critically read in class, portions being memorized"). The third year saw each student required to have a "thorough knowledge of six masterpieces and some acquaintance with about fifty oth-

---

14. *Thirteenth Annual Report*, 18, 136.
15. *Fifteenth Annual Report*, 11.
16. Pollard, *History of the Ohio State University*, 22.
17. *Seventeenth Annual Report*, 16.

ers," which in 1891 included works by Sidney, Spenser, Bacon, Milton, Bunyan, Addison, Pope, Johnson, Goldsmith, Coleridge, Keats, Shelley, Byron, and Browning, through to such near contemporaries as Carlyle and Tennyson. By then, too, American literature was being covered—"the study of American masterpieces with a view to discovering the distinctly American elements and characteristics. The representative authors will be Irving, Poe, Bryant, Whittier, Lowell, Longfellow, Holmes, Hawthorne, and Emerson." The senior year offered "Shakespeare and the English Drama" from "the Miracle Plays down to the present time."[18]

In that year, for some reason the Department was again split in two: into English language and literature, and Rhetoric. The year 1891 also saw the appointment of Joseph Denney, who soon tried to end that division. By 1893 he was recommending—unsuccessfully at that point—"the temporary union of the departments of English language and literature and rhetoric, with a view to greater economy of their management."[19] No such merger took place until 1904, and it was only then that Denney actually taught in (and chaired) the Department of English Literature—the Department to which he would come to seem to have arrived "Moses-like," to "mold a department and a college and thus leave his imprint on the University."[20]

18. Dasher, *A Brief History*, 11–13.
19. Pollard, *History of the Ohio State University*, 126.
20. Dasher, *A Brief History*, 16.

CHAPTER 2

The Length and Shadow, the Lengthened Shadow

The Denney Years

JOSEPH VILLIERS DENNEY (1862–1935) came to Ohio State with a B.A. from the University of Michigan (1885), having worked from 1885 to 1890 as a journalist and then the principal of a high school in Aurora, Illinois; he returned to Michigan for graduate work but never received his degree, until awarded an honorary graduate degree by his alma mater in 1910. He began as an Associate Professor at OSU and was promoted to full Professor in 1894. He became Dean of the College of Arts, Philosophy, and Science in 1901 and was appointed acting President of the University in 1909, all while continuing in his role as Chair of the English Department. He also served as President of the American Association of University Professors from 1922 to 1924. He was instrumental in bringing the thirty-sixth meeting of the Modern Language Association to Columbus, in 1920.[1]

---

1. According to the program of the meeting, it was held "under the auspices of the Ohio State University," March 29–31, 1920; "Shortage of coal and restrictions on travel in the late fall of 1919" caused the meeting to be postponed from December 1919 (iii).

Apparently the program still referred to the originally planned 1919 schedule when it reported that:

> At seven o'clock in the evening of Tuesday, December 30, the ladies of the Association were entertained at dinner at the Hotel Deshler.
>
> At half-past eight o'clock in the evening of Tuesday, December 30, the gentlemen of the Association were invited to a smoker in the Ball Room of the Hotel Deshler. A smoke talk was given by Professor Joseph Villiers Denney, of the Ohio State University. (xvi)

FIGURE 2.1. Joseph Villiers Denney

As the allusion to Moses in Nancy Dasher's admirable history of the Department suggests, it would be difficult to exaggerate Denney's impact on his Department, College, and University, and on generations of students and faculty.[2] At a time when the cachet of "Rhetoric" declined in much of the nation, Denney oversaw its growing importance and prestige at Ohio State, overseeing, for example, changing the title of the first-year rhetoric course to the "Science of Rhetoric."[3] Denney also taught journalism classes, until the creation of the Department of Journalism in 1914.

---

2. As Dasher also puts it—clearly referring, for example, to two Department Chairs, James Fullington and Robert Estrich, and probably as well to herself—"Those still living who worked with or studied under him can testify to his eloquence, his persuasiveness, and his charm (albeit charm not altogether guileless on occasion)." Dasher, *Brief History*, 19.

3. Mendenhall, "Joseph V. Denney," 138. Mendenhall's essay is an excellent account of Denney's career and significance in the profession. She cites Sharon Crowley as noting that "Denney was among the first of many to insist that reading alone would not suffice for writing instruction (92)." Ibid., 139. On Denney's importance to the history of Rhetoric within the Department, see also Andrea Lunsford's account, in chapter 5 of the present history.

But his interests in rhetoric and journalism did not mean he was not also passionate about the importance of literary studies. Some of the offerings during his time are especially notable for their interdisciplinary innovations, such as a two-semester course in "the study of a novel for its dramatic elements," "under the direction of the Professor of English Literature, followed by its recasting in the form of a play under the direction of the Professor of Rhetoric, and its presentation by the Class under the direction of the instructor in Public Speaking."[4]

Among the many undergraduates who had a profound respect for Denney was James Thurber, who would in later years frequently quote Denney's quip, in regard to the priorities of the University, "Millions for manure, but not one cent for literature."[5] Although he never saw Denney at a football game, another remark that Thurber liked to cite was that "there is no forward passing in learning; you have to cover the ground the hard way."[6] He also approvingly quoted the assessment by the Columbus *Dispatch* that Ohio State University was "in large part the length and shadow of Joseph Villiers Denney." Actually, there is a discrepancy, one that has not been noticed before. The *Dispatch* wrote that "every institution is but the lengthened shadow of a man, and Ohio State university is in no small part the lengthened shadow of Professor Joseph Villiers Denney. . . ."[7] The sentence was read to Thurber because of his blindness, and he clearly heard it wrong.[8] In any case, Thurber said that he could not "associate shadow with Joe Denney," but preferred "the word 'light.' He cast a light, and still does—the light of learning, of scholarship, of laughter, of wisdom, and that special and precious light reflected by a man forever armored in courage."[9] Thurber admired Denney's courage against the philistines not only culturally but politically, in standing up for freedom of expression.

---

4. *Twenty-Ninth Annual Report* (1899), 156–157. Annie Mendenhall is not certain that the course was actually offered, but she nevertheless points out that it "represents an innovative attempt to teach rhetoric and to bridge department boundaries." Mendenhall, "Joseph V. Denney," 153.

5. Thurber, *Thurber Album*, 207. The remark, Thurber goes on to report, did not originate with Denney, but with the Iowa author Ellis Parker Butler; "Joe Denney gave him full credit for the crack, but two generations of Ohio Staters insist the professor thought of it first."

6. Thurber, *Thurber Album*, 205; also in his dedication speech for Denney Hall, "He Cast a Light," 7.

7. Editorial, *Columbus Evening Dispatch* (June 21, 1935): 4-A.

8. The "length and shadow" version is quoted in the plaque hanging next to the J. E. Grimes painting of Denney (see the reproduction of the portrait at the end of this chapter).

9. Thurber, "He Cast a Light," 6; cf. id., *Thurber Album*, 212. The chapter on Denney is called "Length and Shadow."

FIGURE 2.2. James Thurber, 1917

Thurber's semesters at Ohio State were at first lonely and unexceptional; he blossomed under the mentorship of his close friend and fellow undergraduate Elliott Nugent. Years later, Thurber and Nugent collaborated on a hit Broadway play, *The Male Animal* (1939). The protagonist, Tommy Turner, is an English professor at Midwestern University, clearly based on Ohio State. The Dean is Dean Damon, just as clearly based on Denney; like Denney, he is both the Dean and the Chairman of the English Department. "He is a tall, thin, distinguished-looking man of some sixty-five years. . . . He talks slowly . . . often hesitates, peers over his glasses before saying the last word of a phrase or sentence."[10] Turner gets in trouble with a member of the Board of Trustees, Edward K. Keller, when he insists on reading with his class a speech by Bartolomeo Vanzetti, of the famous 1920s trial of Sacco and Vanzetti:

TOMMY—He [Vanzetti] was accused of murder, but thousands of people believe he was executed simply because of the ideas he believed in.

10. Thurber and Nugent, *The Male Animal*, 218.

FIGURE 2.3. *The Male Animal,* OSU Production, 1950

ED—That's a dangerous thing to bring up.

TOMMY (GETTING REALLY MAD)—No, it's a dangerous thing to keep down.
I'm fighting for a teacher's rights, but if you want to make it political, all
right! You can't suppress ideas because you don't like them—not in this
country—not yet. This is a university![11]

Coming down on Turner's side is, of all things, a University administrator,
the counterpart of Joseph Denney. Dean Damon says that he is tired of being
"kicked around in this institution by one Edward K. Keller after another";
Keller insists that "there is only one Edward K. Keller," but for Damon "there
has always been at least one. But there is an increasing element in the faculty which resents your attitude toward any teacher who raises his voice or so
much as clears his throat. I warn you that if you persist in persecuting Thomas
Turner, you will have a fight on your hands, my friend."[12]

Nugent played Turner on Broadway; the movie version (1942) starred
Henry Fonda in that role.

It was remade as a banal musical, *She's Working Her Way through College*
(1952), with Ronald Reagan and Virginia Mayo, which trivialized and totally

---

11. Thurber and Nugent, *The Male Animal,* 244.
12. Thurber and Nugent, *The Male Animal,* 246.

depoliticized the original. When the OSU Department of Theatre put on *The Male Animal* in November, 1978, Professor of English and Rhetoric Edward P. J. Corbett played the role of Dean Damon.

A core group of faculty under Denney consisted of the so-called "trinity," or "Denney's boys": Joseph R. Taylor, George McKnight, and William L. Graves, all of whom stayed in the Department until Denney's retirement and beyond. Taylor, as we have seen, was awarded a B.A. in English at the University in 1887. In 1895 he is listed as perhaps the first graduate assistant in the Department, as an "Assistant in Rhetoric." According to the Board of Trustees, "It was found early in the year that the number of students in the department of rhetoric was too large for a single instructor and the needed help was provided by the transfer of Joseph R. Taylor, B.A., from the department of drawing. Mr. Taylor is exceptionally well qualified for his new duties."[13] With Denney and McKnight, Taylor turned out to be one of what James Thurber called, in his speech at the dedication of Denney Hall in April, 1960, the "three favorite English professors of mine": in fact, he was *the* favorite, according to his chapter on Taylor in *The Thurber Album*.[14] The chapter was called "Man with a Pipe," after the painting of Taylor by his protégé, George Bellows, whom Taylor had encouraged to pursue his art professionally. The relationship between Taylor and Bellows is a story of mentorship that could have parallels throughout the history of the English Department, or in many fields in colleges and universities everywhere, if not invariably with a result as successful (or so right-minded):

> The one freshman class that truly changed [Bellows's] life . . . was English literature—not just because of the content but because of the man behind the lectern, Associate Professor John Russell Taylor. . . . A fine scholar, and a published poet, Taylor took a shine to this six-foot-two freshman, kept an eye on him, and eventually gained his confidence. There was some trouble at home, Taylor learned: George, Senior, would not tolerate any talk about his son's unrealistic, impractical career plans. . . .
>
> It was Professor Taylor who advised the young man to stand firm and to keep his hopes alive.[15]

According to Thurber biographer Charles S. Holmes, "For Thurber, Taylor was the embodiment of high intellectual and artistic standards and something

13. *Twenty-Fifth Annual Report*, 6, 28.

14. The speech was published in the *Ohio State Monthly* (May 1960): 6–7; see also, Thurber, *Thurber Album*, 174.

15. Haverstock, *George Bellows*, 20. See also, in the same volume, Joseph Russell Taylor, "On the Death of George Bellows," 151–153.

which answered a deep need in his own youthful nature—the aesthetic view of life. Taylor was a minor poet, a painter . . . a product of the genteel tradition, a devoted feminist, a seeker after beauty in the late Victorian fashion. Henry James was his great hero. . . . Thurber's most obvious legacy from Taylor is his lifelong admiration for Henry James."[16]

Thurber recalled in his speech dedicating Denney Hall (which, because of his near blindness, as we have mentioned, was actually read by his wife, Helen) that his friend Mark Van Doren—himself a Professor of English at Columbia University—was struck by "my fondness for what he called the species known as English professor."[17] Another admired member of that species was George McKnight, a medievalist and philologist with a Ph.D. from Cornell University (1896). Thurber was ultimately less impressed by the third of his three favorite English professors, William L. Graves, "the most popular professor in the history of his university":

> Joe Denney, like Joe Taylor, was loved and admired by the appreciative few, but Billy Graves was known for more than forty years as the friend of freshmen, the confidant of seniors, and the chum of alumni. . . .
>
> When the intellectuals were talking profoundly about "Ulysses" and "The Waste Land," he was still praising the simple beauties of one of his favorite books, "The Inn of the Silver Moon," by a man named Herman Knickerbocker Vielé. Billy Graves, his myriad young friends told people, was a good guy; he could go along with a gag; he was fun to have around.[18]

But things turned sour in later years. In a regular column Graves wrote for the *Lantern*, Thurber reports, "he came out with violent attacks on his once beloved England for having instigated, as he put it, the Second World War, sharply criticized our 'pro-British Congress,' mysteriously discovered the gaiety of Paris under the Germans and the city's relief at the departure of British and American tourists, and praised Charles A. Lindbergh in a brief, extravagant paragraph."[19]

Another of Thurber's close friends was Herman Miller, who also taught in the Department, and to whom Thurber dedicated *The Thurber Album*. In his speech in Denney Hall, he said that "the Department of English is, of course, dear to my heart because of the men I have already mentioned, and one I can-

---

16. Holmes, *Clocks of Columbus*, 29–30.
17. Thurber, "He Cast a Light," 6.
18. Thurber, *Thurber Album*, 186–187.
19. Thurber, *Thurber Album*, 196. James Fullington, the future Chair of the Department and a long-time friend of Thurber, "objected that he had not done justice to Graves." Holmes, *Clocks of Columbus*, 266.

FIGURE 2.4. Painting of Joseph V. Denney
by J. E. Grimes. The painting is now at the
east end of the first floor of Denney Hall.

FIGURE 2.5. James Thurber at the dedication of Denney Hall, April 1, 1960, with the
portrait of Denney behind him. Seated at his right is Novice G. Fawcett, President of
the University; at his left is J. Osborn Fuller, Dean of the College of Arts and Sciences.

not leave out, the late Herman Miller, who meant as much to me as any man who ever lived."[20] The two for a time considered collaborating on a play based on *The Ambassadors*.[21]

Despite Joseph Russell Taylor's passion for Henry James and the fact that he taught American literature in the Department for decades—the course that James A. Chalmers had first offered as early as 1891—that field remained secondary and largely confined to lower-level courses until after World War II.[22] A key document showing Denney's curricular priorities is a letter he sent May 4, 1904, to the Board of Trustees suggesting his "plan for organization of a department of English"—the merger of the departments of English language and literature and rhetoric—a plan that presented "a complete and unified scheme of undergraduate instruction in English" along "four lines of work":

1. **The structure and history of English as a language.** This would include courses in Anglo-Saxon, Middle and Modern English, historical English Grammar and Phonetics. . . .

2. **The history and development of English thought as embodied in English Literature.** This would include . . . the logical development of our national and racial ideas. In these courses comparatively little attention would be paid to form. . . .

3. **The appreciation of works of English and American Literature as works of art.** . . . In these courses literature would be presented from the point of view of aesthetics, and principles of literary criticism would be taught.

4. **The writing of English.** This would include the principles of Rhetoric. . . . In these courses, extending through the four years, the aim should be purely practical and utilitarian.

   This plan is in full accord with the practice of the best American universities in their undergraduate courses. . . . There should be provision also in the graduate courses for the study of comparative literature, for the investigation of the influences of other literature upon English

20. Thurber, "He Cast a Light," 5.

21. Holmes, *Clocks of Columbus*, 114. Herman's papers relevant to Thurber are in the OSU Libraries. In his speech, Thurber names among those who "were great friends of mine and still are" the OSU football legend Charles ("Chic") Harley—who was suffering from dementia and resident at the Veteran's Administration Hospital in Danville, Illinois, where he had spent most of his adult life. Thurber, "He Cast a Light," 7.

22. See the discussion below, and Renker, *The Origins of American Literature Studies*.

Literature and for research work in the sources of English Literature in the various periods of its history.[23]

No specific explanation is provided of what was meant by "our national and racial ideas," but apparently they were in accord "with the practice of the best American universities." The *Record of Proceedings* goes on to report that "President [William Oxley] Thompson recommended that the general scheme outlined in Professor Denney's report be approved, and that the details of the department be left for further development. He also recommended that Professor Denney be designated as the head of the department. . . ."[24]

We can see what these guidelines meant in practical terms by looking at, for example, the English undergraduate course offerings of the College of Arts, Philosophy and Science in 1905–1906. They include the expected courses on Chaucer, "From Spenser to Milton," and "From Dryden to Pope," and so on, but also more recent literature, with separate courses on Tennyson and Browning. There are no fewer than three courses on "The English Bible," the single course in American literature, and even one (also taught by Taylor) on "Current Literature."[25]

Denney resigned as Dean in 1921 but continued as Chair of the Department until his retirement in 1932. By then he had hired a great many faculty in his effort—as Dasher puts it—"to build a great department."[26] Besides those already mentioned, among his appointments were the following:

Edwin L. Beck (n.d., but by 1910), co-editor with Royall Snow of anthologies of Romantic and later poets. He was Acting Chair for two years after Denney.[27]

Gertrude Lucille Robinson, 1913, whose papers, 1913–33, are in the University Archives. She received an M.A. at OSU in 1916 with a thesis on Elizabethan drama. A long-standing award for undergraduates in creative writing is named after her, as was a special collection in the Library of the Department created in 1934. She served as faculty advisor of Chi Delta Phi, a women's honorary group.

---

23. *Record of Proceedings of the Board of Trustees of The Ohio State University from June 30, 1900, to July 1, 1904*, 43–44.

24. *Record of Proceedings of the Board of Trustees of The Ohio State University from June 30, 1900, to July 1, 1904*, 46.

25. *Course Offerings Bulletin* (1905), 36–38.

26. Dasher, *Brief History*, 37.

27. On all these and other faculty appointments, see "Department Staff List from 1911 to 2000.exlsx," https://osu.app.box.com/files/0/f/4178714451/1/f_32190112867.

Milton O. Percival, 1915, a scholar of Victorian poetry and William Blake, and an early writer on *Moby-Dick*.

James F. Fullington, 1916, who received his OSU M.A. in 1923 and his Ph.D. in 1930, and who went on to become Chair and Dean.

Harlan H. Hatcher, 1922, who became President of the University of Michigan in 1951, after having served as Dean of the College of Arts and Sciences and Vice President of the University at Ohio State.

Tom Burns Haber, 1924, a critic and editor of A. E. Housman, and the author of such books as *A Writer's Handbook of American Usage* and, with George H. McKnight (and W. Wilbur Hatfield), of *A Grammar of Living English*.

John Harold Wilson, 1924, a prominent as well as popular writer of many books on Restoration drama. His *Nell Gwyn, Royal Mistress* was a selection of the Book of the Month Club in 1952.[28]

Harold R. Walley, 1925, a Shakespeare scholar and co-editor, with John Harold Wilson, of *Early Seventeenth-Century Plays, 1600–1642*.

Robert S. Newdick, 1928, who received his B.A. at OSU in 1919, and an M.A. and Ph.D. from Harvard in 1920 and 1930. He had been working on a biography of Robert Frost with Frost's cooperation, and had arranged several visits by Frost to OSU, when he died of an attack of appendicitis in 1939. In a 1941 interview, Frost remarked, "Yes, I suppose I killed Newdick. I remember seeing him at Ohio State. . . . I scolded him for digging up my past. . . . I told him I wouldn't stand for it, and he'd have to stop it. It broke his heart and he died. Of course, I didn't exactly kill him. He died during an appendectomy, but I didn't help him any. He died very young." Playwright Jerome Lawrence, who had been Newdick's student, asserted in "An Appreciation" that "If my professional standards as a writer are high, Robert Newdick set the goals."[29]

Royall H. Snow, 1928, editor of anthologies of Romantic and Victorian poetry. Snow was briefly engaged to Martha Dodd, daughter of William Dodd, ambassador in Berlin, in 1930; Dodd is a major figure in Erik Larson's *In the Garden of Beasts: Love, Terror, and an American Family in Hitler's Berlin*.

Wilson R. Dumble, 1928, who received an OSU M.A. with a thesis on John Galsworthy. By the mid-1960s Dumble was still teaching and had a reputation as one of the most popular teachers in the University, especially among members of fraternities, and was considered such an easy grader

28. Wheeler, *Estrich Years*, 2.
29. Newdick, *Newdick's Season of Frost*, 251, ix.

that his courses in the Department were not permitted to be counted toward the major.

William H. Hildreth, 1931, who co-edited with Wilson Dumble a collection of *Five Contemporary American Plays*.

Denney died a few years after his retirement, in 1935. For decades the most prestigious award given by the Department to undergraduates has been the Denney Award, to the Outstanding Senior English Major. A quarter of a century after his death, he was appropriately honored when the new building housing the Department of English was named in his honor. Before then the Department had been housed with little permanence; it was for a time in Mendenhall Laboratory (then called the Physics Building), and then in Derby Hall (then called the Chemistry Building), from which it moved to the newly constructed Denney Hall in 1960. Given the cramped quarters the faculty and staff had been used to, Nancy Dasher no doubt spoke for many at the time when she said that the move "was certainly the occasion of the most rejoicing."[30] It has to be admitted, however, that in later years the building turned out to be one that, in itself, few people would love.

---

30. Dasher, *Brief History*, 63.

CHAPTER 3

Crises and Opportunities

The Fullington Years

THE DEPARTMENT went with an Acting Chairman (Edwin L. Beck) for a couple of years until 1934, and then an Executive Committee (Milton O. Percival, Harold R. Walley, and James. F. Fullington), with Fullington serving as Executive Secretary (1934–37). He was appointed Chairman in 1937, his first year as a full Professor. Over the years, the Department has kept to the tradition of choosing its leadership from within.

Fullington had received his B.A. from the Department in 1916, and he then became a graduate assistant. He volunteered for ambulance service in France in 1917 before the US entered World War I, when he served with the American Ambulance Field Service, earning the Croix de Guerre with two citations. After the war he held several positions in the business world, then resumed his graduate studies, earning two M.A. degrees (from Harvard and OSU), and his Ph.D. from Ohio State in 1930 with a dissertation on the eighteenth-century poet and landscape gardener William Shenstone. At first a faculty member in the College of Education, he transferred to the English Department in 1931.

Even before Fullington became head of the Department, the Executive Committee had already administered "the most significant change of recent years," according to the Board of Trustees,

the thorough revision of the curriculum, which was put into effect in the Autumn Quarter of 1934–35. This involved the cancellation of several courses

21

on the "400," "500," and "600" levels, the modification of others, and the introduction of several new courses. The aim on the "400" and "500" levels was to arrange and integrate a series of courses which would be educationally valuable to the non-English major and which would provide a satisfactory preliminary background and training for the prospective English major. On the "600" level the aim was to provide courses which would adequately cover the vast field without overlapping and to group and relate the courses in English language and literary history so that the student's chosen course of study could be made significant. To assist in this aim, the system of "Cycles" was inaugurated, so that in the senior year the English major would be required to spend at least a portion of his time in a consistent program of concentration.[1]

Around this time, the Department also faced the rising pressure to incorporate more recent literature into the curriculum. Beck, Hatcher, Walley, Fullington, and Percival authored a report, "Framing an English Curriculum," which stated:

> One of the most difficult questions in the construction of an entire curriculum is the position of contemporary literature. Two generations ago this problem did not exist. Philology was in the saddle, and the Middle Ages was its stamping ground. Little by little, however, as the philological ideal weakened, later literature asserted itself, until today the literature of the present and the recent past threatens to dominate the entire curriculum.[2]

Note the term "threatens": but in fact the threat, if such it was, was postponed for some years.

All these pressures and changes came at a time of great stress not only in the Department but of course in the University and the entire nation, as the hardships of the Depression continued and in some ways even intensified. Yet somehow Fullington was able to oversee some of the most significant faculty appointments the English Department has ever had.

A notable example—dating, actually, from the regime as it were of the Executive Committee—is Francis Lee Utley, who joined the Department in 1935 and was one of its most prominent faculty members for decades. He was the author of a great many articles, notes, and pamphlets in various fields, and

1. *Sixty-fifth Annual Report*, 39.
2. Quoted in Renker, *Origins of American Literature Studies*, 117. Renker's book, which contains a full chapter on Ohio State, is an enlightening account of American academic literary studies that has value beyond its focus on American literature.

of *The Crooked Rib: An Analytical Index to the Argument about Women in English and Scots Literature to the End of the Year 1568* (1944). He edited *The Forward Movement of the Fourteenth Century* (1961), and was the co-editor, with Lynn Z. Bloom and Arthur Kinney, of *Bear, Man, and God: Seven Approaches to William Faulkner's The Bear* (1964). Two of his former graduate students, Jerome Mandel and Bruce A. Rosenberg, edited *Medieval Literature and Folklore Studies: Essays in Honor of Francis Lee Utley* (1970).

As the title of that volume might suggest, Utley was a central figure in the development and growth of two important fields within the Department: folklore and medieval studies. We will pursue the area of folklore in chapter 5, in a section authored by Patrick Mullen and Amy Shuman, but now we get ahead of ourselves by providing an account of the role of Medieval and Renaissance Studies within—and without—the Department.

MEDIEVAL AND RENAISSANCE STUDIES

Not entirely ahead of ourselves, however. For, as we have already indicated, the study of texts in Old and Middle English languages and literatures—and their relationships to other languages and literatures—was a long-standing academic strength in the Department, and Anglo-Saxon studies were a part of the original curricula from the nineteenth and early twentieth centuries on, as they were at many universities. Any number of courses taught the English language by also teaching its Anglo-Saxon origins and development.

Then, in the 1950s, largely led by Utley, whose view of medieval studies was a broad one, interested scholars within the University—from the Department and from Art History, History, and Music—began to enjoy a flourishing association that comprised one of the best interdisciplinary programs in the country. A "Medieval Club," consisting of members from several disciplines, began in 1956 to meet about once a quarter at private homes or the Faculty Club. In 1958, they sponsored a conference, "Aspects of Late Medieval Art," which led to the publication of Utley's edited volume *The Forward Movement of the Fourteenth Century.*

In 1966, following encouragement and financial support from the newly established National Endowment for the Humanities and with support from the growing cadre of medievalists across OSU's College of Humanities, the Center for Medieval and Renaissance Studies was established. Utley was chair of its coordinating committee and oversaw the search for a permanent director. Stanley J. Kahrl, from the University of Rochester, and a student of prominent medievalists at Harvard (where Fullington as well as Utley had trained), was chosen and arrived at OSU in 1969. Utley and Kahrl approached medieval studies from different angles, all of them valuable for interdisciplinary activity—Kahrl an authority on the study of war as well as its literature, and Utley a multidisciplinary critic and folklorist. Kahrl believed deeply in outreach and public education, as was apparent in his contributions to the Medieval Academy's committees and regional associations' activities and his involvement in the Civil War movie *Glory,* for which he recruited African American student actors from Ohio State. Indeed, Kahrl died unexpectedly while attending a Civil War reenactment in Tennessee.

Because medievalists of whatever stripe need to know Latin as well as other texts that their ordinary reading may not touch on, for years a medieval reading group and a Medieval Latin practice group, kept active and directed by Lisa Kiser, strengthened faculty and graduate student learning through informal gatherings. Kiser brought her notable scholarship to bear as well in editing for some years *Studies in the Age of Chaucer,* the journal sponsored by the New Chaucer Society, the organization overseen for a time by Chris Zacher. More of the CMRS directors—Kahrl, Zacher, Nicholas Howe, and Richard Greene among them—have been medievalists than their Early Modern and Renaissance colleagues. Because of that, the CMRS has sought to engage those non-medievalists in various ways, pedagogical and scholarly. The figure of Shakespeare and the Renaissance world around him have always naturally loomed large in such efforts, as did Chaucer in the earliest curricula.

Shakespeare has been a presence for a range of colleagues through the annual or smaller Center conferences—such as William Baillie, Lee Sheridan Cox, David Frantz, John Gabel, Ruth Hughey, Robert Jones, Rolf Soellner, and Harold Walley, just as George McKnight in the early part of the century was known for his studies of Chaucer and Arthurian literature. Prominent and lesser-known medieval authors were the focus of studies by, for example, Alan Brown, Drew Jones, Kahrl, Kiser, Ethan Knapp, Leslie Lockett, Walter Scheps, Martin Stevens, Karen Winstead, and Zacher.

Fran Utley's broad view of the Middle Ages would lead his colleagues to undertake such projects as hosting the annual meeting of the Medieval Academy and, in 1992, an array of scholarly and popular events highlighting the Christopher Columbus Quincentenary, both during Zacher's term as CMRS director. Utley was the first person to receive a Guggenheim Fellowship while in the Department (Ruth Hughey was awarded one before coming to OSU).[3] He was a great friend of the University Libraries, and after his death a fountain in his name was erected within the Thompson Library, at the main entrance. When some years later the fountain was removed during renovations, the

---

3. Other recipients have been John Harold Wilson (1950), Robert Elliott (1962), Morris Beja (1972), James Kincaid (1973), Richard Altick (1975), Leslie Tannenbaum (1982), Amy Shuman (1989), Andrew Hudgins (2004), and John King (2009).

plaque—mentioning both Fran and his wife Scotty—was moved to the fourth floor, near room 450. And in a Department in which many faculty have had their own notably large libraries, Utley stood apart. A familiar campus sight was of Fran or one of his graduate students carrying bags of books to and from the Library—students who might also serve as bartenders at the frequent Utley cocktail parties. He and Scotty eventually had to move from their large Clintonville home to an even larger house in Upper Arlington (appropriately on Coventry Road, near Chaucer Drive), in the basement of which were "stacks" reminiscent of those in the Thompson Library, housing more than 30,000 volumes. Anyone who browsed through the stacks confident that no one could actually read all those books would pick up a volume at random and find Utley's marginalia throughout. He had promised Scotty that if he could buy all the books he wanted, she could have a fur coat. She got the coat.

Also hired in 1935 were William Riley Parker and James V. Logan, Jr. Parker wrote a major biography of John Milton and important criticism about his work; among his other publications was the 1951 edition of *The MLA Style Sheet,* then a small pamphlet that "expanded the consensus" for style and formatting among journal and book publishers.[4] He had left OSU to become the editor of *PMLA* in 1946; the annual prize for the outstanding article in *PMLA* is named in his honor. Upon leaving the MLA, he joined the Department of English at Indiana University. Logan, a critic and scholar of Romantic poetry, retired in 1977.

Ruth Hughey, who would in 1957 become the Department's first female full Professor, was appointed by OSU in 1938 as the Elizabeth Clay Howard Scholar, and then in 1939 as an Assistant Professor. As recorded by two of her nieces for the "Emory Women Writers Research Project," "born in 1899 in rural Arkansas, Ruth Hughey was the eldest daughter of a Methodist minister and his wife, both college graduates. When she was two years old she was stricken with polio, leaving her severely crippled and requiring braces on both legs and crutches to walk." She received her B.A. from Galloway College in 1920 and went to New York to pursue graduate studies at Columbia without being formally admitted. Eventually allowed into the program, she was awarded an M.A. but could not afford to pursue the Ph.D. After several years teaching in Arkansas, she enrolled in Cornell, where she received her Ph.D. in 1932 with a dissertation on "Cultural Interests of Women in England from 1524 to 1640 Indicated in the Writings of the Women." After a stint on the faculty of Mount Holyoke, she came to Ohio State: "Her office was on the third floor

---

4. *MLA Handbook: Eighth Edition,* x.

FIGURE 3.1. Francis Lee Utley

of a building without an elevator. She climbed the stairs several times a day managing books and crutches without assistance."[5]

She edited *The Correspondence of Lady Katherine Paston, 1603–1627* (1941) and published, with the Ohio State University Press, *The Arundel Harington Manuscript of Tudor Poetry* (1960) and *John Harington of Stepney, Tudor Gentleman: His Life and Works* (1971). Although she was not above seventy when she retired in 1969, inevitably she seemed old to her admiring graduate students. As one former student marveled to us, "she remembered seeing Pavlova dance around 1905 when she was a schoolgirl."[6] Again, her nieces: "She died at the age of eighty, leaving a legacy of research on previously unknown women writers. Her determination to herald their literary talent, which for centuries had gone unnoticed, mirrored her own struggle to survive and prevail in a culture unfriendly to brilliant, scholarly women. Like those women before her, she was heroic in refusing to let the outside world define her limits and her identity."

William Charvat joined the Department in 1944. By then the University had postwar plans for an interdisciplinary program in "American Civilization," plans which, as Elizabeth Renker points out, largely came about as the result of "the extramural forces of nationalism during World War II. American lit-

---

5. Laney and Reilly, "Family Reflections."
6. Martin Beller, email, July 15, 2015.

FIGURE 3.2. Ruth Hughey

erature would finally receive an enthusiastic curricular embrace at Ohio State
at this time. Ironically, because of the practical services it could render in the
cause of nationalism, it even outpaced the status of the field of English that
had consistently marginalized it."[7]

Charvat was already a prominent figure in studies of American culture
and literature, and especially of the history of American publishing. *The Origins of American Critical Thought, 1810–1835* (1936) came out of his 1934 dissertation at the University of Pennsylvania. The University of Pennsylvania
Press published *Literary Publishing in America, 1790–1850* in 1959, and the
OSU Press published *The Profession of Authorship in America, 1800–1870* in
1968. The William J. Charvat Collection of American Literature in the University Libraries is one of the most important in the world, especially but not
exclusively in holdings of 1901–25.

The OSU Press had also started the *Centenary Edition of the Works of
Nathaniel Hawthorne* in 1962, with Charvat, Roy Harvey Pearce, and Claude
M. Simpson, all in the Department, as General Editors, and Matthew J. Bruc-
coli, also in the Department, as Associate Textual Editor. (Fredson Bowers

---

7. Renker, *Origins of American Literature Studies*, 9.

FIGURE 3.3. William J. Charvat

of the University of Virginia was Textual Editor.) Among the "Sponsors for the Ohio State University" was "The English Department, Robert M. Estrich, *Chairman.*" In 1976, Thomas Woodson of the Department joined the edition as its historical editor. As Woodson has noted, the Hawthorne edition "was the first of a score of editions that have since become associated with universities and their presses all over the country," and represented at its start "a novel approach to scholarship, presenting a concentrated effort to republish masterpieces in the most accurate texts possible, recreated if necessary from manuscripts and various compared editions to present the author's final and best intention."[8]

Pearce had come to the Department the year after Charvat, in 1945, and Simpson in 1947. Both achieved prominence in American studies: for example, Pearce with *Savagism and Civilization: A Study of the Indian and the American Mind* (1953) and *The Continuity of American Poetry* (1961); and Simpson with *The British Broadside Ballad and Its Music* (1966). And both were to become part of the exodus to the new California system in the 1960s: Simpson to

---

8. Woodson, "Center for Textual Studies," 4.

Stanford in 1964, and Pearce in 1963 to help found the Literature Department at the University of California, San Diego—together with Robert Elliott, who had been hired in 1946, and Andrew Wright, hired in 1949. Don Howard left for the University of California, Riverside in 1962.

In 1945, the Department hired Richard D. Altick, who was to become among the most internationally prominent of all its scholars during his years at Ohio State—the rest of his entire career—at which he was awarded the title of Regents Professor. He had come to the University from a position in the faculty at Franklin and Marshall, where he had obtained his B.A. in 1936 (he earned his Ph.D. at the University of Pennsylvania in 1941); he retired in 1982. He made clear the joy and excitement he found in his work in *The Scholar Adventurers* (1950), in which he told fascinating stories of scholarly discoveries about the works of a number of major authors. His influential textbook, *Preface to Critical Reading* (1946), appeared in many editions, including one co-authored with Andrea Lunsford (1984). Among his many other widely known books are *The English Common Reader: A Social History of the Mass Reading Public, 1800–1900* (1957); *The Art of Literary Research* (1963); *The Shows of London* (1978); *Paintings from Books: Art and Literature in Britain, 1760–1900* (1985); and, co-written by his former student and then colleague, James F. Loucks II, *Browning's Roman Murder Story: A Reading of The Ring and the Book* (1968). Two other colleagues, James Kincaid and Albert J. Kuhn, co-edited *Victorian Literature and Society: Essays Presented to Richard D. Altick* (1984), published by the Ohio State University Press, which also published a number of Altick's own books, such as the one for which he received the Modern Language Association's Christian Gauss Award for the best book of literary scholarship or criticism, *The Presence of the Present: Topics of the Day in the Victorian Novel* (1991),[9] and on the Board of which he was very active.

Within the English Department, Altick was no doubt most known for his famous—or infamous—course, English 980, Bibliography and Method, required of all Ph.D. students and notorious for how demanding and difficult it was. In the responses requested of Ph.D. alumni for a Departmental self-study conducted in 1978, the comments about what one former student called "R. Altick's demon of a bibliography course" were paradoxical but emphatically positive; only two responses were negative, while twenty-three cited it as the most valuable course they had taken. A footnote to the self-study reads: "Professor Altick, having read the above paragraph in an earlier draft of this report, adds: 'That this course has continued to be required of Ph.D. candi-

9. The Christian Gauss Award had been previously won by Joan Webber in 1963, for *Contrary Music: The Prose Style of John Donne*.

FIGURE 3.4. Richard D. Altick

dates despite the perennial complaints from students that it is over-demanding and/or irrelevant has always seemed to me a prime instance of the department's academic integrity. Not all English departments would steadfastly sustain a course whose value evidently becomes apparent to many students only after the passage of a number of years.'"[10] Upon Altick's retirement, the course was taken over by John Gabel—once a student in the course—who naturally taught it very differently, and then, with the growing importance of the Web and digital sources, by James Bracken, of the University Libraries. Finally, Altick's comments about the Department's steadfastness notwithstanding, the requirement for the course was waived in 1988.

Margaret Blickle, hired in 1945, became a pioneer within the Department in the field of business and technical writing, co-editing with her colleague Martha E. Passe *Readings for Technical Writers* (1968) and co-authoring with another colleague, Deborah C. Andrews, *Technical Writing: Techniques and Forms* (1978). Blickle also held various administrative posts within the rhetoric and composition program. Another significant person in the history of

10. Beja et al., "Report of the Self-Study Committee," 42.

rhetoric and composition within the Department was someone not actually in the field: Edwin W. Robbins, hired in 1948 after his Ph.D. from the University of Illinois; the Illinois Press published the book based on his dissertation, *Dramatic Characterization in Printed Commentaries on Terence, 1473–1600*, in 1951. Robbins served for many years as the director of what was then called freshman composition. He retired in 1981 and moved to North Carolina; he died in 2001.

The linguist and medievalist Morton W. Bloomfield came to the Department in 1946. He soon published *Canadian English and Its Relation to Eighteenth Century American Speech* (1948) and other important works, such as *The Seven Deadly Sins: An Introduction to the History of a Religious Concept, with Special Reference to Medieval English Literature* (1952); *Essays and Explorations: Studies in Ideas, Language, and Literature* (1970); and, with Leonard Newmark, also in the Department, *A Linguistic Introduction to the History of English* (1963). Newmark left OSU to join Pearce, Simpson, and Wright at San Diego, and Bloomfield went to Harvard in 1961; Harvard sponsors the Morton W. Bloomfield Lectures in his honor.

Emmanuel Varandyan, a native of Armenia, joined the Department in 1949. His novel *The Well of Ararat* had been published in 1938; another novel, *The Moon Sails,* appeared in 1971. But he did not teach creative writing within the Department. The Colombian-born philosopher and critic Eliseo Vivas had a joint appointment with the Department of Philosophy (perhaps the first such joint listing) from 1949 to 1951.

The present authors must also mention our gratitude and debt to Nancy Dasher, who began as an undergraduate in 1926, and started her graduate studies in 1931. She became an Assistant Professor in 1963. Her 1970 mimeographed history of the Department has been invaluable to us. She was also recognized for her important professional contributions by the College English Association of Ohio, which has annually presented, since 1979, the Nancy Dasher Award for outstanding publications by faculty from CEAO departments in "creative writing, professional and pedagogical issues, and literary scholarship and criticism."

It would of course be impossible to name all the students who came through Ohio State University during Fullington's time as Chair (and difficult to name all the faculty, for that matter), but the story of one student, perhaps arbitrarily, stands out. We get to that student with a flash forward. In 1988, while working on a project on James Joyce, Morris Beja re-read Noel Riley Fitch's *Sylvia Beach and the Lost Generation* and again came across a reference to Joyce's having received, in Paris, a letter from Columbus, Ohio, from someone who described himself as "an unheard of student" named Sam Steward,

FIGURE 3.5. Nancy Dasher

requesting Joyce write to the OSU Library asking that the student be permitted to borrow *Ulysses*; he had so far been denied that permission[11]. (The novel was of course at that time still banned in the United States, but sure enough the Library acquired its first copy in 1926.) As Chair of the Department, Beja had access to names and addresses of alumni, and found a Dr. Samuel M. Steward—now living in Berkeley—who had received his B.A. in 1931, as well as an M.A. and a Ph.D. in 1932 and 1934, all from the English Department. Without doing his homework, on an impulse Beja picked up the phone and called him—and Steward answered on the first ring.

They had a pleasant chat—Steward had been receiving the Department newsletter, *Impromptu,* so to that degree he had been in touch with what had been going on. It turned out that if Beja had known his literary history a bit more, he would have been aware that Sam Steward was a friend of Gertrude Stein and Alice B. Toklas and that their letters to him appear in *Dear Sammy* (1977). Steward had also published a great many books, including *Chapters from an Autobiography* (1981), and a number of novels, including many of

---

11. Fitch, 251.

gay erotica under the *nom de plume* Phil Andros (such as *$tud,* 1966, and *Joy Spot,* 1969).

In his autobiographical writings Steward tells how, at Ohio State, he and his friends "read Dreiser and Anderson and Hemingway, sat through endless hours of O'Neill tragedies, read smuggled copies of Joyce's *Ulysses,* adored Garbo and Stravinsky," and so on.[12] He was later fired from what was then the State College of Washington at Pullman because, he says, he had published a "racy novel with a street walker in it," *Angels on the Bough,* which he had written while at Ohio State.[13] He also taught at Loyola in Chicago, but "after twenty years of university teaching, I gave it all up to become a tattoo artist."[14] And he did, too.

When Gertrude Stein came to the States on a lecture tour in 1934, after the successful publication of *The Autobiography of Alice B. Toklas,* she wrote to Steward from the Deshler-Wallick Hotel: "I liked your Columbus a lot, it is an xceedingly pleasant Columbus, and I am glad the first University understanding I ever had came from there." She credits Clarence E. Andrews (to whom Steward also pays tribute) with having been "the first man connected with the teaching of English in an American University who took any interest in me."[15] (Andrews had been hired by Denney in 1915 and taught in the Department until 1933. He was a poet, critic, and fiction writer. His *Innocents of Paris,* 1928, was adapted—loosely—for Maurice Chevalier's first film in 1929.) Later, in 1939, Stein wrote, "When they ask but why did you want to go back to U. S. I always say because I want to see Columbus Ohio again. . . ."[16]

Steward and Beja kept in touch intermittently, and when he died in 1993, Steward bequeathed $40,000 to the Department. Those funds helped in putting on a conference, "Queer Places, Practices, and Places: A Symposium in Honor of Sam Steward," in May 2012, coordinated by Debra Moddelmog, then the Co-Director of the Sexuality Studies program and Co-Organizer and Director of the Diversity and Identity Studies Collective at OSU ("DISCO"), and, later, Chair of the Department.

By the way, Joyce never did answer Steward's letter.

Another student surely worth mentioning is the Department's first African American Ph.D. student, Charles Eaton Burch, who received his doctorate in 1933 with a dissertation on "The English Reputation of Daniel Defoe." He had been teaching at Howard University and returned to it and soon became

---

12. Steward, *Chapters,* 21.
13. Steward, *Chapters,* 39.
14. Steward, *Chapters,* 79.
15. Steward, *Dear Sammy,* 122.
16. Steward, *Dear Sammy,* 143.

Head of the Department of English. In addition to his ongoing work on Defoe, Burch initiated an intensive program in African American literature and folklore together with the distinguished scholar Sterling A. Brown. When Burch died in 1948, Howard University sponsored the Annual Charles Eaton Burch Memorial Lecture, which is still thriving.

Records in this area are far from complete, but on September 13, 1971, then Chair John Gabel responded to a request by the Office of Minority Affairs with a list of the Department's known African American Ph.D. recipients; the following all received graduate degrees while Fullington was Chair. William Edward Farrison received the Ph.D. in 1936 with the dissertation "The Phonology of the Illiterate Negro Dialect of Guilford County, North Carolina." He went on to publish *William Wells Brown: Author and Reformer* with the University of Chicago Press in 1969. Farrison taught at North Carolina Central University from 1938 to 1962, and was Chair for a number of years. The campus building in which the English Department is housed is named the Farrison-Newton Communications Building, after him and another member of the faculty, Pauline Newton.

H. Alfred Farrell earned an M.A. in 1939 and a Ph.D. in 1947. He taught at Lincoln University, Pennsylvania, where he had earned his B.A., until his retirement in 1984; he had chaired the English Department for seventeen years. The Department's first African American female Ph.D., we believe, was Iva Jones, who received her M.A. in 1943 with a thesis on "Percy Bysshe Shelley as a Reformer" and her Ph.D. in 1953 with her dissertation, "A Study of the Literary Reputation of Anthony Trollope, 1847–1953." Carl Marshall received his M.A. in 1947 with a thesis on "William Cullen Bryant's Literary Criticism," and his Ph.D. in 1954; his dissertation was titled "American Critical Attitudes toward the Fiction of William Dean Howells." He became a faculty member at the Lima campus and after several administrative posts joined the Columbus campus in 1971 as the Department's first African American full Professor, retiring in 1982.

The Depression of course produced problems for the entire University: students, faculty, and administrators. But efforts were made to help, and among the most innovative that Fullington came up with (working with Beck, Hatcher, Percival, Walley, and Wilson) was the creation of the English Department Library in 1934.[17] Housed at first on the second floor of Derby Hall and then in its basement, the EDL levied a small fee for students of introductory literature courses, but in return loaned them all the books needed for the courses, saving students the major expense of purchasing

---

17. Dasher, *Brief History,* 40.

such books—so that, for example, the library had scores or even hundreds of copies of Conrad's *Lord Jim*. It was also a reading room, stocked with a great deal of contemporary literature that the Main Library could not afford to purchase in those years. Eventually the EDL also housed the Robinson Memorial Collection, named after Gertrude Lucille Robinson in honor of her work, for example, with Chi Delta Phi, the women's honorary society; the Herman A. Miller Drama Collection, initiated by Miller's own books and plays; and the Teaching Aids collection, for assistance in teaching freshman composition.

At first the acting librarian was a graduate student (Margaret Foster), until Clarene Dorsey was hired in 1940; she retained that post until her retirement in 1976. The records of the Board of Trustees announcing that appointment give her name as Clarence—surely not the only time she suffered that indignity.[18] According to information Dorsey supplied to Nancy Dasher, "as of June 30, 1965, the Library had 15,221 books (not counting 'text' duplicates) and 86 periodicals";[19] but it was shortly after that time that budgetary restrictions led to the Library being unable to make any purchases at all, so it became, really, a reading room. During the mid-1980s it began to be used as the Department's default site for lectures, until finally the University claimed the space, in return for which it combined and renovated two classrooms in Denney Hall, 311 and 313, creating the English Department Commons Room. The University Libraries took over almost all the books, although the Department kept some, including the copies of faculty publications that had also been part of the collection.

During many of the years of the existence of the EDL, the University Libraries also staffed the English, Theatre, and Communications room in the Thompson Library, which consisted of reference and reserve books, and periodicals. Faculty and graduate students also used it—the "ETC"—as an important reading room.

The crises caused by the Depression were followed by those resulting from World War II. Enrollments throughout the University declined precipitously; the Department had fifty-six faculty/staff positions in 1941, forty-one in 1944.[20] Those problems were then followed by strains created by the huge influx of students into the University after the war—from 6,500 in 1943 to 25,400 in 1947[21]—all of them required to "take English." Nancy Dasher reports, "Long-time staff members (including the writer) still talk about those days when they

18. http://trustees.osu.edu/assets/files/minutes/Archive%20minutes/1940-1943.pdf, p. 6.
19. Dasher, *Brief History*, 51.
20. Dasher, *Brief History*, 54.
21. Shkurti, *Ohio State in the Sixties*, 4.

FIGURE 3.6. James F. Fullington, 1945

taught sections of Freshman English in left-over Army 'shacks,' about the size of an old-fashioned voting booth and heated by a gas burner, placed squarely in the middle of the room—a system of heating that was generally 'too much' or 'too little.' The staff was recruited from here, there, and everywhere, and Mr. Fullington had to 'scrape the bottom of the barrel' so often that even the barrel threatened to give way."[22] Once again, crises led to opportunities and innovations. In the early 1950s the Department created its first formal Honors program, and the first program for speakers of other languages, directed initially by Robert M. Estrich, who had in 1946 become the Department's first Vice Chairman, and in fact the first Vice Chairman of any department in the University.

Fullington became Dean of the College of Arts and Sciences in 1951, and Estrich effectively assumed the Chairmanship. When major violations of Western Athletic Conference rules were discovered within the OSU football program in 1955, the Faculty Council created a special committee, chaired by Fullington, to investigate intercollegiate athletics at the University. After more

---

22. Dasher, *Brief History,* 56.

than two years, the "Fullington Committee" issued its sweeping report, out of which, for example, came the creation of the Athletic Council:

> Among its twenty-one recommendations were that "[a]t no time shall the unique advantage of football be considered license for expenditures out of balance with other sports" and that "as long as coaches hold rank on the faculty they should take part in academic life. . . ." . . . Athletes should have tutors from academic departments directly. . . . It called for replacing the Athletic Board, to which the president appointed faculty members, with an Athletic Council whose faculty members received appointments from Faculty Council and who reported to Faculty Council. . . .
>
> Most importantly, the Fullington Committee called for recognizing that the traditional ideal of the amateur athlete in intercollegiate competition was out of date. ". . . it is foolish to expect the program can continue at that level [$2,000,000 a year] without letting the athlete in for some portion of the gain either as an inducement for him to come or as aid to him as a resident student."[23]

Upon his return to the English Department, Fullington taught the course in the Bible as Literature (a course subsequently taught, also with great popularity, by, among others, Robert Estrich, John Gabel, Charles Wheeler, David Citino, and Arnold Shapiro). Just before his retirement, James Fullington received one of the University's first Alumni Distinguished Teaching Awards, in 1965.

---

23. Goerler, *Illustrated History*, 207. Other members of the Department have continued to play important roles in the governance of University athletics over the years. Al Kuhn, Julian Markels, and David Frantz have all chaired the Athletic Council, and Chris Zacher and Beverly Moss have served on it; Moss also followed Frantz in the role of Academic Liaison with Athletics in the early 2000s. See also the account of the role of sports in the Department by Frantz in chapter 5.

CHAPTER 4

Primus inter Pares

The Estrich Years

AFTER FULLINGTON left the chairmanship, Robert M. Estrich (pronounced "east-rye") was effectively the Chairman for thirteen years, from 1951 until 1964. Having been raised on a farm in northeastern Ohio, he joined the Department as a graduate student, and Graduate Assistant, in 1928. His dissertation (1935) was on Chaucer. Although his only published book would be *Three Keys to Language* (1952), co-authored with Hans Sperber of the German Department, no one could doubt how learned he was. His mentoring of his colleagues, junior and senior, whatever their field, was legendary. As Charles Wheeler has testified, for Bob Estrich "the lives and careers of his colleagues were paramount. People came to Estrich with their troubles. He held their hands. He dispensed advice and consolation. He read their manuscripts and annotated them as well. He kept their secrets." Julian Markels speculates that "he had more books dedicated to him, and more eloquent acknowledgements, than anybody in the profession of his generation and maybe since."[1]

Estrich's collegiality extended to the very frequent parties that he and his wife, Alice, would host at their home. It was in fact a time when there were numerous parties in the Department—just about weekly at someone's home at least during fall quarter. English was a drinking department, and at the parties the hosts would pour manhattans and martinis (Estrich especially loved

---

1. Wheeler, *Estrich Years*, 10, 23.

FIGURE 4.1. Robert M. Estrich

martinis) seemingly incessantly, and have other hard liquor available at a bar. Those who went to such parties during the 1950s and 1960s have urged the authors of this history to make sure we mention the parties, and the drinking, and how amazed they (and we) are at how, after all that drinking, people would as a matter of course just get in their cars and drive home. Estrich could certainly hold his own liquor, and did: he had, one noted very soon upon meeting him, the face of an apparent drinker. Both Julian Markels and Dick Altick, in their contributions to the reminiscences of Estrich edited by Wheeler, refer fondly to Estrich's "bulbous nose," as well as to his "red" or "ruddy" complexion.[2] He continued his strong imbibing into retirement, often lunching with former colleagues (like Chris Zacher) over martinis that sometimes led to a meal.

Senior professors were also collegial in encouraging junior faculty to lunch at a regular spot in the Faculty Club; Estrich would often be there, as would Utley, Wilson, and Robbins, for example. Later regulars would include, in addition to faculty from elsewhere in the University, Ed Robbins, Ed Corbett,

---

2. Wheeler, *Estrich Years*, 23, 36.

Charles Wheeler, David Frantz, Dan Barnes, Matt Bruccoli (for a while: more on his relationship to Department collegiality in the next chapter), Jim Kincaid, Arnie Shapiro, David Citino, Dick Martin, Tom Cooley, Sara Garnes, Rolf Soellner, Walter Scheps, Melanie Lusk, Steve Fink, Susan Miller, Sebastian Knowles, the authors of this history, others perhaps less regularly—and John Gabel, who was so regular that the gathering spot came to be called, to his intense annoyance, the "Gabel Table." The rhyme made the designation inevitable, but the table might also have been named after Corbett—who, as the group on some days became too large for the Club's own table to accommodate everyone, paid for another, larger one to replace it—as a small plaque on the table still attests.

The purpose was not so much to eat as to talk. And at talking Estrich was a master. He *loved* to talk; faculty didn't walk into his office figuring they would get out in a few minutes. Addressing them fondly as "*mon frère*," he would ask them about all kinds of aspects of their lives, and talk about his as well, professional and personal. Charles Wheeler records how, one year, the new faculty, disturbed at the level of their salaries, "asked for an audience with Estrich. What he did was take us, the whole group of new Instructors, to lunch at the Faculty Club, where we sat at a round table in the southwest corner of the dining room and ate and talked. Or rather, Estrich talked. He *talked*. The words flowed out with hardly any interruption . . . until finally it was 1:30 in the afternoon and we were the only customers left in the dining room. As we rose and made our way stiffly to the exit, we felt that somehow the problem had been resolved, while at the same time we were aware that no raises had been promised us that year—and indeed, that none were forthcoming. For some reason, it didn't matter."[3]

Within his office, conversations with Estrich had one element of discomfort: in his time there was no dividing wall between the Chair's desk and area and the desk and area of his assistant, Alyce Moore. Alyce Moore was a profoundly formidable presence in the Department and often enough a deeply troubling and scary one. She controlled course schedules, and had no hesitancy in assigning someone who had crossed her an 8:00 a.m. class. Sitting at her desk with a cigarette in her mouth she heard everything that went on between you and the Chair—everything. The participants in the Department's periodic poker sessions invented a particularly grueling game with complicated and hard-to-master rules; it was called "Alyce Moore." As Richard Altick

---

3. Wheeler, *Estrich Years*, 8–9.

reports, "She cowed even the most bumptious of the new faculty; it was of her that Roy Harvey Pearce once observed, 'A. Moore vincit omnia.'"[4]

All that put a certain edge to the knack Estrich had of making you feel comfortable, though in the end that knack wasn't truly diminished. In support of Charles Wheeler's anecdote it can also be reported that the junior faculty used to say that Bob Estrich could get you into his office, make you feel terrific and loved, and you would eventually leave and be halfway down the hall before you realized you had just been fired.

Not before, in those days, you had proven your mettle by teaching English 690 (later 699), a "capstone" course required of all English majors. It was taught in small sections of half a dozen or so students; in addition to the seminar meetings, each student met with the instructor in a private "tutorial" once a week. Content centered on the "canon," represented by a two-to-three-page reading list (from, say, "The Second Shepherds' Play" to *Middlemarch* to "The Love Song of J. Alfred Prufrock" and, perhaps, *The Sun Also Rises*), a list that the faculty vehemently debated each year. The debates in those days didn't center on whether there was or should be a canon, but on what constituted that canon, and on which works could be squeezed into the list. With the idea of a canon assumed, the goal was to fill in—during the ten weeks of the quarter—each student's "gaps." Determining whether that was achieved was the task of a common exam at the end of the quarter, taken by all the students in all the sections of the course, and graded by all the teachers. The fact that it was a requirement for the major meant that students could not graduate without at least a C in the course. Students were duly petrified, and the faculty nervous as well. The course finally disappeared, an inevitable casualty of the "canon wars."

In the early sixties, new faculty Ph.D.s were still hired as Instructors, not Assistant Professors. Estrich changed that by the mid-sixties, to compete with the hiring practice of other universities; those already hired as Instructors were promoted, but they were still on the same tenure clock. At the senior level, Estrich also ended a long-standing practice that no one could be paid a higher salary than the Chairman.

The Department had "a long tradition of hiring only people for whom a tenured position would be open following their probationary appointment."[5] That was far from the universal procedure or policy in academe. But life was not easy for those striving for tenure. All new hires at the beginning level taught at first three sections per quarter of "Freshman Composition." A

---

4. Wheeler, *Estrich Years*, 39.
5. Markels, *From Buchenwald*, 127–128.

FIGURE 4.2. Charles B. Wheeler

sequence of three quarters of composition was required for almost all first-year students; it was not until the third quarter that readings became mostly "literary." Until tenured, faculty taught nine courses per year. Eventually, the standard "teaching load" was five courses; the quarter with only one course was one's "light" quarter. One could also apply for a quarter free of teaching; an advantage of the quarter system was that, while competitive and far from assured, such "research" quarters were a bit easier to attain than they would have been under a semester system.

One of Estrich's earliest hires was Howard Babb, the author of two books published by the OSU Press: *Jane Austen's Novels: The Fabric of Dialogue* (1962) and *The Novels of William Golding* (1970). He was promoted to Assistant Professor in 1957 and Associate Professor in 1962; he left as part of the exodus to the California system in 1965.

Charles B. Wheeler and A. E. Wallace Maurer were both hired in 1953. Wheeler published *The Design of Poetry* (1966) and, co-authored with John Gabel, *The Bible as Literature: An Introduction* (1986), which went into many editions. He was also a poet. For four years, he served as Estrich's Executive Secretary, a position similar to that of Vice Chairman.

Maurer was the editor of two volumes in the University of California Press edition of *The Works of John Dryden: Prose, 1668–1691: An Essay of Dramatick Poesie and Shorter Works* (1971) and *Prose 1691–1698: De Arte Graphica and Shorter Works* (1989). He was a gifted pianist—a notable example of a tradition of especially talented musicians within the Department, such as, coming after Maurer, Dan Barnes, Suzanne Ferguson, Sara Garnes, and Sebastian Knowles. A charming eccentric, Wally would strew mounds of papers all over the floor of his office, until required by the fire marshals to stop. He was also famed (one has to acknowledge, to some extent notorious) for his habit at lectures of volunteering to ask the first question, which would often turn out to be long, complicated, and not easy to follow or respond to. A small plaque in honor of that tradition was placed on a seat in the front row of the Commons Room, where most Department lectures take place, at the memorial service after his death in 2016 at the age of ninety-four. He had fought his forced retirement twenty-four years earlier. The University ended its policy of compulsory retirement at the age of seventy just too late for Wally, who had to retire in the last year of the old rule, 1992. With the vigorous support of the Department, he appealed for a reversal or exception in his case, but without success. He was, apparently, the last person at The Ohio State University to be forced to retire because of his age.

Albert J. Kuhn, whose years as Chair will be the subject of our next chapter, was hired as an Instructor in 1954, promoted in 1957 and then again in 1961 to Associate Professor; he became Chair (or "Chairman") in 1964, and was promoted to full Professor the next year. In 1971 he was appointed Acting Vice President for Academic Affairs by President Novice Fawcett and then named Provost by President Harold Enarson. After his return to the Department, he became Director of the University's Honors program; he retired in 1991. With James Kincaid, he edited *Victorian Literature and Society: Essays Presented to Richard D. Altick* (1984).

Donald R. Howard came to OSU in 1956, was promoted in 1958 and in 1962, and left for the University of California, Riverside, in 1963, again as part of the Department losses in that era to the California system. Among his books are *The Three Temptations: Medieval Man in Search of the World* (1966); *Writers and Pilgrims: Medieval Pilgrimage Narratives and Their Posterity* (1980); and *Chaucer: His Life, His Works, His World* (1987). With his Ph.D. advisee Christian Zacher, also from the University of California, Riverside, he co-edited *Critical Studies of Sir Gawain and the Green Knight* in 1968, the year Zacher came to Ohio State. In 1992 Zacher co-edited, with James M. Dean, another Howard student, a festschrift in memory of Howard after his death.

FIGURE 4.3. Albert J. Kuhn, 1955

Another future Chair hired by Estrich was Julian Markels, in 1956; he was promoted in 1960, in 1963, and to full Professor in 1967. Combining interests in American literature and William Shakespeare, he has published *The Pillar of the World: Antony and Cleopatra in Shakespeare's Development* (1968); *Melville and the Politics of Identity: From King Lear to Moby-Dick* (1993); and *Negotiating an Audience for American Exceptionalism: Redburn and Roughing It* (1999). Julian was married for a time to a colleague, Joan Webber (see below); after their separation he married Robin Bell (see the section on sports in the next chapter for how they met). Julian has given an account of his life and career in *From Buchenwald to Havana: The Life and Opinions of a Socialist Professor* (2012), which we will continue to have opportunities to cite a number of times in this history.

The short story writer and novelist Peter Taylor joined the Department in 1957 and left five years later. The author of many story collections, including *Happy Families Are All Alike* (1959), he won the Pulitzer Prize in 1987 for his novel *A Summons to Memphis* (1986).

Gordon K. Grigsby was hired as an Instructor in 1957 as an Americanist and promoted in 1963 and then in 1966 to Associate Professor (the same year

FIGURE 4.4. Julian Markels

he received the University Alumni Award for Distinguished Teaching). He switched gears and published his first volume of poetry, *Tornado Watch,* with the OSU Press in 1977; on the strength of a number of poetry collections he was promoted to full Professor in 1987. In retirement, he started the Evening Street Press, which publishes the *Evening Street Review* and volumes of poetry, fiction, and non-fiction. He died in 2017.

John M. Muste came to OSU in 1958, and was promoted in 1962, 1967, and 1971. His pioneering study, *Say That We Saw Spain Die: Literary Consequences of the Spanish Civil War,* appeared in 1966. He served as Associate Dean of the College of Humanities under Dean G. Micheal Riley until his retirement in 1986. The son of the renowned political activist A. J. Muste, John came down with polio as a young man, during his honeymoon trip to Mexico with his wife, Jean. His crutches never seemed to hamper his activity; James Kincaid speaks for others when he remarks that one of his fondest memories of Ohio State is "Muste's deep gruff kindness—clanking down the hall to see me when I was in my first years." Upon his retirement, the College created the annual John M. Muste Dissertation Prize for the best Department dissertation.

FIGURE 4.5. John M. Muste

Another Americanist, Eric Solomon, also came to the Department in 1958. He published one book on Stephen Crane with the OSU Press (*Stephen Crane in England: A Portrait of the Artist*, 1964) and another with Harvard (*Stephen Crane, from Parody to Realism*, 1966). For his account of why he left Ohio State in 1964, see below.

Estrich's casual openness to hiring Jews into the faculty was not entirely popular with at least one or two of his senior colleagues. Four Jews were hired in 1961, including Jerome Mintz, a folklorist who left after one year.

Frances Ebstein had been an undergraduate at Ohio State. She received her Ph.D. from Indiana University, where she had met Arnold Shapiro, who was also given a faculty appointment two years after Fran (see below); when they married and had children, Fran continued teaching on and off, but not on the tenure track.

Jonathan Baumbach came to the Department from Stanford; his critical dissertation became his first book, *The Landscape of Nightmare: Studies in the Contemporary American Novel* (1965), but from then on he concentrated on his own fiction. Several of his novels have been published by the Fiction Collective, of which he was one of the founders. He left OSU in 1964 for New

York University, but within a few years went on to Brooklyn College for the rest of his career.

Morris Beja was the third future Chair hired by Estrich. He came from Cornell without yet having finished his degree; the Department was able to be patient for a year or so in a way that the University and College would not allow in later decades. One day he was having a pleasant conversation in the coffee room with John Harold Wilson—Jim Wilson. After half an hour or so, there was a pause in the talk and Wilson leaned forward and said to him, "Jonathan, do you know when Murray Beja is going to finish his dissertation?"

When it finally came out, Beja's dissertation was revised to become *Epiphany in the Modern Novel* (1971). Other books include *Film and Literature* (1979), *James Joyce: A Literary Life* (1992), and *Tell us about . . . A Memoir* (2011). He has edited a scholarly edition of Woolf's *Mrs. Dalloway* as well as several volumes of essays on James Joyce, including one co-edited with his wife, Ellen Carol Jones, *Twenty-First Joyce* (2004). She and he have also co-edited *Cinematic Narratives: Transatlantic Perspectives* (2018). Ellen had received her B.A. and M.A. at OSU (and a second M.A. and her Ph.D. at Cornell). Beja has also published the collection *Psychological Fiction* and volumes on Virginia Woolf, Samuel Beckett, and Orson Welles. He edited the *James Joyce Newestlatter* from 1977 to 2017. He founded the International Virginia Woolf Society and was President of the International James Joyce Foundation. He was the first faculty member (as distinct from University administrator) to serve as Chair of the Board of the OSU Press. He had visiting professorships at the University of Thessaloniki, Greece; University College Dublin; and, after retirement, at Northwestern University and Beijing Foreign Studies University. He also spent a term giving several lectures in Japan, where Ellen was a visiting professor at Ferris University, Yokohama.

Beja, who received the University Alumni Award for Distinguished Teaching in 1982, was promoted to Associate Professor in 1968 and to full in 1971. Before coming to OSU but after accepting the position, he was with his then wife, Nancy, in New York, and at the Out of Town Newspaper Stand in Times Square they asked for a Columbus paper. They were given a recent *Dispatch* (March 31, 1961), and went to a nearby cafeteria to read it. When they came to the editorial page, they were struck by an editorial ("More Serious Than Antics") vehemently attacking the Ohio State University Department of English. It seemed that "a certain instructor in the English department" had arranged a visit by a speaker, William Mandel, who had been a "defiant" witness before the House Un-American Activities Committee: "Not all our disgust over shenanigans in the academic field should be directed against cavorting, destructive, bed-pushing students. Some faculty members invite it, too."

Welcome to Ohio State.

FIGURE 4.6. Morris Beja

Which brings us to the Speakers Rule (or Speaker's Rule). As Raimund Goerler summarizes in his history of the University:

> During the 1950s and early 1960s the Speaker's Rule was a flashpoint of conflict between students, faculty, and administration. Originating in 1946 and revised in 1951, the Rule required that students who wished to bring speakers to campus had to request approval from the Office of the President. The trustees who created the rule wanted to prevent OSU from hosting speakers who were perceived as Communists or subversives. . . .
>
> Year after year, students and faculty seethed against the Speaker's Rule and challenged it regularly by inviting controversial speakers to visit the campus.[6]

One context for the controversy was the conservative politics of central Ohio at the time ("Columbus is one of the three most reactionary cities in the United States," Eric Solomon was to claim in the *Atlantic*).[7]

---

6. Goerler, *Illustrated History,* 94.

7. Solomon, "Free Speech," 64.

Mandel was barred from speaking on the campus, whereupon an English Department graduate assistant, Henry St. Onge (Ruth Hughey's Ph.D. student), invited the speaker and the crowd who had gathered to hear him to his nearby backyard on Woodruff Avenue. Despite pressure, Estrich did not deem that just cause for St. Onge to be fired. But the Nebraska college that had offered St. Onge a faculty position backed away from the offer and refused to honor it; again resisting pressure, Estrich employed him for the subsequent year. He eventually moved to a commune in New Zealand.[8] One of those who came to St. Onge's defense was Gordon Grigsby, who was chair of the Central Ohio Chapter of the American Civil Liberties Union.

Things came to a head in April 1962, when President Fawcett cancelled a meeting at which there were to be several speakers invited by Students for Liberal Action. (Ironically, one of the invited speakers was Philip A. Luce, who within a few years became a prominent right-wing spokesman.) Protests over the cancellation led to the largest faculty meeting ever held at the University, and the first in the twentieth century, on May 14, at Mershon Auditorium.

Although the exact figures were often disputed, it turned out that the faculties of arts and science, of law, of education, of engineering, and so forth, were in the minority in the university, where nearly eight hundred agricultural extension workers, county agents, and the like had faculty appointments, and where hundreds of private M.D.'s taught as little as one hour a week in a clinic—often to qualify for football tickets, since the 83,000-seat stadium was always sold out: all were voting faculty. The word went out; the campus was filled with strangers asking the way to the auditorium.[9] The word, moreover, was that attendance had been mandated for the agricultural agents and the adjunct medical faculty.[10]

8. "Knowing all that made me react with some anger to a throwaway passage in E. L. Doctorow's *Book of Daniel*, in which we're told that in the 1950s someone at Ohio State had been fired for teaching *The Catcher in the Rye*. That was absurd, of course; I wasn't here then, but I knew it couldn't have happened under Estrich; I checked with people who *had* been here, and they all said no such event occurred." Beja, in Wheeler, *The Estrich Years* 33. The source of the story may have been a controversy actually entailing the Columbus city schools: "The tensions . . . flared up with particular intensity in Columbus during the 1963–64 school year. It began in October when local activists pressured the city schools to remove from library reading lists books they described as 'filthy, blasphemous, revolutionary or anti-white.' The offending books included J. D. Salinger's *The Catcher in the Rye*, George Orwell's *1984*, and Harper Lee's *To Kill a Mockingbird*. Ohio State was not directly affected, but many students, faculty, and administrators had close ties to the public schools and rallied to the district's defense." Shkurti, *Ohio State in the Sixties*, 106.

9. Solomon, "Free Speech," 72.

10. Markels, *From Buchenwald*, 102.

President Fawcett opened the meeting with a thirty-five-minute speech. He then recognized Richard H. Bohning, Assistant Dean of the College of Agriculture and Home Economics, who made a motion endorsing Fawcett's action. "I think the motion I am about to submit is one to which we can all subscribe," he said, and then produced a roar of unintended laughter when he added that he hoped "the action can be taken with dispatch."[11]

The Department of English loomed large in the opposition to the motion. Andrew Wright pointed out that the call to the meeting had not mentioned voting "on the conscience of the president"; he pleaded that the meeting not force a vote on such a measure and argued that "bringing this motion to a vote would be to make a deep wound that would take many years to heal":

> If The Ohio State University—despite its magnificent achievement, despite its very high rank among the universities of the world, despite its still very great promise—is to turn back the clock and become, as it has been from time to time in its history, a paradigm of paternalism: then of course many members of this faculty will feel compelled to accept the by now notorious invitation to move on. . . .
>
> I am a native of this city and I have deep roots here. My grandfather was a professor at the old Starling-Ohio Medical College and then in the College of Medicine . . . and I myself am a graduate of Ohio State. . . . [If], I say, I should feel compelled to accept the invitation to move on, then I should have to tear up some very deep roots, and to turn my back on a University to which I have given, and given happily, fifteen years of my life.[12]

Wright moved that the motion be tabled; that motion was seconded by W. Todd Furniss, also of the English Department, but it failed by a voice vote. The vote on the original motion was taken: first there was a voice vote, and then a vote in which all eligible faculty stood, for or against. The vote was 1,036 to 509 in favor of the motion, but there was no doubt which "side" the regular faculty of the University was on; "the five hundred who stood to oppose his action, while the students cheered, included nearly the entire heart of the teaching faculty, many chairmen, even some deans—the entire English department, for example. As I watched the smile fade from President Fawcett's face, I realized the meaning of the term 'poleaxed' for the first time."[13]

---

11. "Largest Faculty Meeting," 18.
12. "Largest Faculty Meeting," 13, 18.
13. Solomon, "Free Speech," 73.

Estrich then rose to defend freedom of speech, pleading for "discussion so free that we need not risk being told that we may seek our futures elsewhere if it is denied here."

> I have been teaching at this University for 34 years. Time and time again in those years we have all been harried, and the university's proper business of education interfered with, by problems of freedom of speech on the campus. Early in my time here they involved faculty freedom. . . . Today we have, I believe, no longer any problems of *faculty* right to teach and to speak with genuine intellectual freedom. . . . There still remains to us, however, the acute problem of the right of our faculty and students to hear on-campus speakers from outside the institution. . . .
>
> Of course there are problems (in today's world). But how are they to be solved? Specifically, how are we who teach at The Ohio State University going to accept the obligation laid on us to educate young men and women to solve them?
>
> There is only one way—the way fought for and won by science, the way fought for and won by medicine—free discussion, *totally* free discussion.
>
> We in the faculty have in our classrooms a magnificent intellectual freedom. You, Mr. President, as one of us, have helped us to solidify that freedom. We cherish it as you do. But we cannot truly educate our students unless we give it to them. They are not children. They are not the citizens of the future. They are citizens now. Let us help them to as rapid a maturity and as rich an intelligence as we can.[14]

Even relatively new members of the faculty—for example, those who had not been faculty long enough to be eligible to vote, and who were relegated to sit with the students in the balcony of Mershon, and who were in relative ignorance of campus politics and the realities of power at a university—recognized that for a Chairman to speak against the President was an act of impressive courage and integrity.

In the same spirit of Estrich's remarks, Foster Rhea Dulles of the Department of History moved that "the Faculty of The Ohio State University hereby affirms its full support for the right of free speech on this campus for guest speakers . . . free from restraint or intervention by administrative authority." But Mars G. Fontana, Chairman of Metallurgical Engineering, moved that the meeting be adjourned. The non-debatable motion passed by a voice vote.[15]

Fawcett and the powers that be recognized what had happened. By 1965 the Speakers Rule was history.

---

14. "Largest Faculty Meeting," 14, 18.
15. "Largest Faculty Meeting," 14.

Harm had been done, however. One instance of the negative national attention paid to the University at the time was Eric Solomon's article in the *Atlantic* giving his personal account of what had happened. It started out by asserting that "I liked and admired my colleagues, was satisfied with the library, was more than satisfied with my chairman,"[16] but stressed for example the number of English Department faculty—including, by the way, Andrew Wright, who had spoken at the meeting—who left the University because of the controversy. Actually, although there is no doubt that a number of members of the Department left OSU in part or in large part because of the atmosphere created by the Speakers Rule, it would also be naïve not to recognize the career considerations that led to many or even most of those moves. The burgeoning of the California system, and the high opinion at those universities of the OSU faculty, were huge factors in Ohio State's losses; six of the faculty members leaving the Department in the early 1960s left for California.

There was no question that the losses disturbed Robert Estrich deeply, but he actively continued to hire new faculty. Matthew J. Bruccoli also came in 1961, achieving quick promotions—to Associate Professor in 1964 and full the year after that. Chiefly known as a bibliographer and textual editor, he was a major collector—especially of items relevant to F. Scott Fitzgerald—and the author of *Some Sort of Epic Grandeur: The Life of F. Scott Fitzgerald* (1981). He edited letters and works by Fitzgerald, Hemingway, Stephen Crane, and other American writers. Primarily noted for his work in American literature, he nevertheless was one of the original editors and founders of the *Dictionary of Literary Biography,* an international project of some four hundred volumes.

In time he became one of the most controversial—even legendary— members of the Department. We'll postpone the major aspects of controversy until the next chapter, but we can mention here that for good or bad he was one of the most colorful and outspoken faculty members in the history of the Department. He was both dapper—always dressed impeccably in expensive suits—and gruff, unconcerned with surface politeness. An example those who were there have not forgotten: at lunch at the Faculty Club with a group that included Ed Corbett, Bruccoli became so exasperated with some of Corbett's comments that he said, "Goddamn it, Corbett, you are either the smartest or the dumbest son of a bitch I've ever known, and I'm damned if I know which!" and then proceeded to stub out his cigar in Corbett's salad.

At the elegant dinner parties that he and his wife, Arlyn, hosted, Bruccoli somehow thought it still appropriate, as dinner ended, to excuse all the women while the men were to stay behind to smoke cigars. He seemed unable

---

16. Solomon, "Free Speech," 63.

FIGURE 4.7. Arnold Shapiro

to care less (or to comprehend) how angry that made his guests; one who reacted with icy fury was Joan Webber.

Webber was hired in Renaissance literature in 1962; she was promoted to Associate Professor two years later and to full Professor in 1969. She was the author of *Contrary Music: The Prose Style of John Donne* (1963), which received the Christian Gauss Award given by Phi Beta Kappa for the best book of literary scholarship or criticism; *The Eloquent "I": Style and Self in Seventeenth-Century Prose* (1968); and *Milton and His Epic Tradition* (1979). She was married for a time to Julian Markels; she left Ohio State for the University of Washington in 1972. Joan died in a rock-climbing accident in 1978. In 1980, Washington established in her honor the annual Joan Webber Award for Outstanding Teaching by Graduate Students.

Lee Sheridan Cox, also in Renaissance literature, came to OSU in 1964, was promoted to Associate Professor 1968, and to full Professor 1973. Her *Figurative Design in Hamlet: The Significance of the Dumb Show* appeared in 1973; she had already published a young adult novel, *Andy & Willie: Super Sleuths* in 1967, expanded from "A Simple Incident," which won an award in 1955 as the best short story in *Ellery Queen's Mystery Magazine*. Cox retired in

1983. She remained in Columbus until 2011, then moved to Indiana. She died in 2013 at the age of ninety-six.

Arnold Shapiro joined the Department in 1963 as a specialist in Victorian literature and was promoted to Associate Professor in 1969. In addition to Victorian literature, he taught the Bible as literature and American Jewish literature. He received a Fulbright Lectureship to teach at the University of Helsinki, Finland. Shapiro served for a number of years as Vice Chair of the Department, being especially active in the hiring of new personnel, retiring from that post in 1992. He also for a number of years edited the Department's newsletter, *Impromptu*. He died in 2013.

Thomas Woodson taught at Williams College for two years before coming to Ohio State in 1963; he was promoted in 1969 and 1974. He served as a General Editor of *The Centenary Edition of the Works of Nathaniel Hawthorne* and edited *The French and Italian Notebooks* and *The Consular Letters*. Woodson was President of the Nathaniel Hawthorne Society and received the House of Seven Gables Hawthorne Award for Hawthorne Scholar of the Year in 1991. He held a Fulbright Lectureship at the University of Pau, France, 1968–69. He was Chair of the Comparative Studies Department at OSU from 1975 to 1977. He retired in 1995 and died in 2014 after a bout with Alzheimer's Disease.

Estrich's term as Chair saw major developments in an important aspect of the Department and the University: the role of the regional campuses, a role that John Hellmann outlines for us.

HISTORY OF THE REGIONAL CAMPUSES

John Hellmann

The regional campuses were created starting in the late 1950s and expanded in the 1960s. The campuses at Marion and Newark were established in 1957; those at Mansfield and Lima in 1958 and 1960, respectively. The campuses at Mansfield, Lima, and Newark were greatly enlarged in the late 1960s. All were established with the mission of increasing access to the University for undereducated regions of Ohio. The central administration therefore wanted to establish a true faculty of The Ohio State University at the campuses, with regional faculty members part of their home departments, which would function as the tenure-initiating units. The English Department informed new tenure-track hires that they would be held to the same qualitative research standards as their peers in Columbus, a standard which at that time was articulated as coming up for tenure with a "good book" published or accepted for publication by a good press. The only major program allowed at the regional campuses, however, was in elementary education, and thus the regional faculty in the 1970s and 1980s pursued tenure and promotion within a somewhat contradictory situation: the publishing expectations of a major research university, but teaching opportunities consisting solely of composition and general education requirements. In addition, while all senior faculty members participated in promotion and tenure meetings, neither the small numbers of senior faculty at the regional campuses, nor the traditions and habitual practices of the Department, accorded them a consistent voice in Department deliberations and policies.

Two major changes during the 1990s created the circumstances compelling a solution to this contradiction. A select number of major programs of The Ohio State University were added to the curriculum that could be pursued from start to finish at a regional campus. One of them was English. The offering of the four-year major program in English required an expansion in the number of faculty, with careful attention to various areas of specialization. It also meant that more compelling arguments could be made within the Department for searching for faculty who could meet the highest expectations in research and teaching in their areas of specialization. Thus the establishment of the four-year English major gradually led to the second important change: greater involvement of the faculty on the campus in Columbus with the faculty on the regional campuses. As the regional faculty grew in number and research productivity, they became a significant presence in the Department's promotion and tenure meetings. They effectively became a force that needed either to be fully trusted in their professional judgment, or to be excluded from the deliberations concerning their Columbus-campus colleagues. Two main issues needed to be resolved: 1) should the standards for regional faculty be the same or different? 2) what, if any, should be the roles of regional faculty on Department committees and governance, and what, if any, should be the roles of Columbus faculty in regional programs? As the Department moved into the 2000s, a sizeable new generation of tenured and promoted senior faculty was arriving at the status of senior faculty at the same time as a new generation at the Columbus campus. The relations among faculty across the campuses were generally characterized by a mutual respect for having met the same expectations for tenure and promotion.

Indeed, that new status of the regional-campus English faculty was apparent in the many articles published by them in prestigious journals and books at such major university presses as Columbia and Cornell; the prestigious national research grants awarded to them from organizations such as the American Council of Learned Societies; the major national awards in a regional-faculty member's field, such as one book being named best in the entire field of composition, and another faculty member being named top scholar in her field; the several senior Fulbright Lecturer awards to nations such as Belgium, Poland, and Germany; and the promotion of a regional-faculty member to Full Professor, along with the promotion to Full of three others sometime after they had each transferred to the campus in Columbus. As the research performance of regional-campus faculty became comparable to that of Columbus-campus faculty, and their presence stronger in faculty meetings, the Department seemed to have reached a new equilibrium among the campuses as the second decade of the new century approached.

With the conversion of the University calendar from the quarter system to the semester system, however, new factors threatened that equilibrium. Whereas on the quarter system regional English faculty taught a six-course load and the Columbus faculty a five-course load, the central administration now decreed that regional faculty would continue to have a six-course load while Columbus faculty would have a four-course load. The exact scope of this widened discrepancy in teaching load was difficult to determine, since undergraduate courses at the regional campuses were usually capped for a smaller enrollment. Nevertheless, tenure standards and the role of regional-campus faculty within the Department became once again a matter for discussion, with the pressure of a higher teaching load presenting concerns about the ability of probationary faculty to meet the same standards as those of faculty in Columbus. This developing situation also raised concerns among some Columbus faculty about the role of regional faculty in some Department deliberations. While the principle of the same qualitative minimum standard in research continued, as well as the basic expectation of a "good book" at tenure, some slight modification of the quantitative standard was enacted to reflect the disparity in teaching load for faculty at the regional campuses.

Yet the momentum that had been achieved over the previous decades remained a powerful force. Today, the regional campuses have a high-quality faculty with national and international reputations in their fields. They bring access to The Ohio State University to place-bound students and students who desire a smaller-college experience, and they also function as a gateway for Ohioans whose admittance to the Columbus campus is postponed for two semesters. Expanding opportunities at the regional campuses enhance the pursuit of the traditional English degree: advanced courses in a number of fields, a focus on study abroad, research and honors opportunities, training and experience as writing tutors, and new programs such as the minor in professional writing and its related community internships. Many graduates of The Ohio State University continue to obtain their degrees with a major in English by taking courses wholly or in large part at the regional campuses. Several English majors at the regional campuses have won the Department's highest annual awards, including the Robert E. Reiter Prize for Critical Analysis, awarded to the best essay written in any OSU English course during the preceding year, and the Denney Award for Best Graduating Senior. For these reasons, the history of the Regional Campuses has been a story of progress and of significant contribution within the life of the Department and the communities of their respective regions.

Changes in governance also occurred at the Columbus campus during Estrich's term as Chair. First, he extended the consultation with the faculty from conferring with full Professors to Associate Professors as well—the "Senior Staff." But then came the Executive Committee. As Julian Markels reports:

> Soon after being awarded tenure in 1961, I began my Ohio State career of political activism by proposing revolutionary change in the structure and process of English department government. . . . The Senior Staff met twice a month for lunch at a long table in the Faculty Club, where Bob Estrich sat at the head and transmitted the university administration's latest directives, along with the latest rumors about the legislature's mood, the forthcoming deanship vacancy, and the construction schedule for our new building. It appointed the departmental committees and reserved to itself the power to approve of committee proposals.[17]

By the mid-1960s, Department governance—although not in regard to matters of promotion and tenure—had largely shifted to a new "Executive Committee." At first it consisted of the Chair, the Chair of the Graduate Committee, the director of Freshman English, and two elected members from each of the three professorial ranks (each serving a two-year term); eventually it also included representatives from among Instructors and graduate and undergraduate students. Its activities and duties included preparing the agenda for meetings of the general Department (the "English Department Council"); serving as a committee on committees and coordinating the work of the various Department committees; advising the Chair on priorities for new personnel; hearing grievances; and generally consulting with the Chair on matters of policy.

The result was a change in the role of the Chair. In the traditional nomenclature, although the title as such was not used, Denney and Fullington, and so on, had been the "Head" of the Department. Perhaps not always completely comfortably, as Charles Wheeler conjectures, Estrich was "*primus inter pares*, elected by and answering to the faculty."[18]

---

17. Markels, *From Buchenwald*, 100.
18. Wheeler, *Estrich Years*, 14.

At the same time, the Department's place within the overall University structure shifted. A committee appointed by President Fawcett in 1959 issued its report in 1962. As summarized by William Shkurti,

> The committee, chaired by veteran English professor James Fullington, focused on the dysfunctional structure of OSU's liberal arts core, which was scattered by happenstance and history throughout a number of different colleges. Economics and sociology were housed in the College of Commerce, psychology in the College of Education, and biology and botany in the College of Agriculture. In most other top universities these disciplines were consolidated into an arts and sciences college.
>
> Ohio State's College of the Arts and Sciences was already too big, and adding more departments would not work. Instead the committee recommended four smaller, more nimble colleges clustered around the humanities, physical sciences, life sciences and social sciences.[19]

When this reorganization eventually came about in the mid-sixties, the Department of English, of course, was placed within the College of Humanities.

Among the graduate students of the 1950s was the future bestselling novelist John Jakes (the author of the *American Bicentennial* series, and *North and South,* for example), who writes that upon his arrival on campus in 1952, "it was made clear to us that the principal function of graduate assistants teaching first year classes was to flunk out students. At that time Ohio law said that any high school graduate could attend OSU, no questions asked."

> Several professors stand out in memory. I had never before encountered Chaucer, and Dr. Francis Utley brought him alive in our seminar, roguishly rolling his eyes as he relished some of the racier passages. Dr. [Harold] Walley was a bold and theatrical purveyor of Shakespeare. My thesis adviser was Dr. Louis Simpson, who let me plow ahead with a study of novels of World War II, though I still harbor an uneasy feeling that he didn't think too much of my qualifications to be an academic.

When Jakes let it be known that he had published stories in some "science fiction pulps," Jackson Cope, then an Instructor in the Department before he moved on to Johns Hopkins, "called me to his office and, behind his closed door, politely informed me that my pulp tales weren't 'the kind of thing' the

---

19. Shkurti, *Ohio State in the Sixties,* 70.

FIGURE 4.8. The Chairs, as of 1986: Julian Markels, John Gabel,
Robert Estrich, Albert J. Kuhn, Morris Beja

OSU English department was looking for. . . . This incident allowed me to convince myself that I wasn't cut out for the academic life."[20]

Robert Estrich resigned as Chair in 1964 and retired in 1971. In 1990, funds from Alice Estrich, colleagues, friends, and former students created the annual Estrich Award for the best paper by a graduate student in the Department of English, to recognize how "he was instrumental in transforming the department into both a model within the university and a national presence in the academic profession."

In 1986, the then-still-living Chairs assembled at Friendship Village, the retirement facility in north Columbus where Bob and Alice were living. As Charles Wheeler reports, part of the purpose of the visit was

to set up a group portrait of Bob together with Al Kuhn, Julian Markels, John Gabel, and Murray Beja, the last the current Chairman and the others former Chairmen of the Department. Bob seemed quite pleased by the attention, though he didn't say much. I am happy that this recognition came at a

20. John Jakes, letter to Debra Moddelmog, February 25, 2016.

time when he could still appreciate it, and that I, as the photographer, was able to be a part of it. The year was 1986; he died in 1989.[21]

When she died in 1992, Alice—who had made astute investments in stocks—left a bequest of $3.2 million dollars to the Columbus Foundation, to benefit efforts to help victims of abuse, the terminally ill, family planning services, and other programs for the needy.

---

21. Wheeler, *Estrich Years*, 20–21.

CHAPTER 5

The Troubles

The Kuhn Years

ALBERT J. KUHN (the Chair from 1964 to 1971) is remembered as a man of perception, intellect, and courage, and with a great deal of quiet dignity—and also as someone who, at parties, would happily spin women around (the same fellow who, at one party during a game of charades, turned beet red when asked to act out the phrase "Modess because . . ."). Jim Kincaid writes:

Al was the oddest chair I've known—with some endearing traits (most evident to me only later, when he and I edited the volume honoring Dick Altick). He threw a cocktail party, fall 66, to start the term. Being uncouth and nervous, I got there about ten minutes before 5 (the announced starting time), a full hour before everyone else. About pissing myself with anxiety, I spent the time drinking martinis (or some such) and getting roaring drunk. I remember little, apart from lecturing Ed Robbins on the true meaning of Milton's poetry—ALL of it. The following Monday, deeply abashed, I went to Al to apologize. Stranger than strange, he came around the desk and hugged me.

Very sweet—and uncommon, I think. Al was a hugger from way back, but, so far as everyone knew, only at parties, when drunk, and women were present.[1]

---

1. Letter to the authors, February 11, 2016.

FIGURE 5.1. Albert J. Kuhn

One of Kuhn's earliest popular decisions as Chair was to erect a partition—a wall, really—between his desk and Alyce Moore's, providing a sense of confidentiality to conferences with the Chair that had hitherto been lacking. And when Moore retired, he replaced her with young Michael Rupright, a graduate of the Department's M.A. program, who remained an admired and accessible Assistant to the Chair until his own retirement in 1994.

Among Kuhn's first appointments was the medievalist Martin Stevens, who came in 1964 as an Associate Professor and was promoted the next year. Stevens was a critic and textual editor, of for example *The Towneley Cycle* and *The Canterbury Tales,* and the editor and author as well of a number of volumes of criticism and scholarship. He left the University in 1969 and became Chair at the CUNY Graduate Center.

Richard T. Martin was hired in 1964 as an Assistant Professor who taught Romantic poetry and was promoted with tenure in 1970; he retired in 2000.

John B. Gabel received his Ph.D. from Ohio State and went on to the University of Illinois. The Department brought him back in 1965 as an Associate

FIGURE 5.2. John B. Gabel

Professor. His term as Chair will be the focus of our next chapter, although before that he served as Acting Chair when Kuhn had a sabbatical research year in London, 1971–72. With Carl C. Schlam he published a Latin edition and English translation of Thomas Chaloner's *In Laudem Henrici Octavi,* and with Charles Wheeler he published *The Bible as Literature: An Introduction,* which has gone through numerous editions. He also wrote *The Jennings Years, 1981–1990* (1992), the volume on the presidency of Edward Jennings for the ongoing *History of the Ohio State University.*

Also hired in 1965 was the Renaissance scholar Robert C. Jones; he was promoted to Associate Professor in 1971. He suffered a debilitating stroke in 1985, while serving as the Department's Director of Graduate Studies. The Department and the College managed to arrange a research leave that helped him to retire that year. He moved to New Mexico, and in retirement published two books: *Engagement with Knavery: Point of View in Richard III, The Jew of Malta, Volpone, and The Revenger's Tragedy* (1986) and *These Valiant Dead: Renewing the Past in Shakespeare's Histories* (1991).

FIGURE 5.3. Robert Canzoneri

Our account in this history does not profile each and every faculty member ever hired by the English Department. In particular, we do not discuss most of those who were not awarded tenure or who left OSU within a short time for whatever reason. But of course it must be acknowledged that in retrospect some of the Department's tenure decisions may seem questionable, at the very least in terms of achieved scholarship. One example may be that of Gerald Bruns, a modernist and critical theorist who was hired in 1965 and was eventually denied tenure, but who went on to a stellar career, first at the University of Iowa and then at the University of Notre Dame, where he became the William P. and Hazel B. White Professor of English and was elected to the American Academy of Arts and Sciences.

An important appointment for the history of the Creative Writing program was that of Robert Canzoneri in 1965, as an Associate Professor; he was promoted in 1969 and retired in 1991. Originally from Mississippi (with a Ph.D. from Stanford), he published *"I Do So Politely": A Voice from the South* the year he came to OSU. Other works of nonfiction include *A Highly Ramified* Tree (1976). He also wrote fiction, including the novel *Men with Little*

Hammers (1969) and *Barbed Wire and Other Stories* (1970). He was one of ten members of the "Committee of Inquiry" that, in November 1970, produced the 238-page report, "The Spring Events at Ohio State." And he was the first director of Creative Writing in the Department.

Of course, there had been other creative writers in the Department before that. The literary magazine *Gifthorse: A Yearbook of Writing*, was published by the Department in the 1940s, with poems and stories by students and also by faculty, including Harold R. Walley and Royall Snow. Al Kuhn writes about one creative writer, Emmanuel Varandyan, in his informal memoir, "Words in Time":

> [Varandyan] came to us from Michigan in the 1940s, where he had won a prestigious prize. Of Armenian descent, he wrote out of that cultural background on what I recollect as fairly exotic subjects. He was not a distinguished nor a flexible teacher, and his writing was sporadic, so that his colleagues found him unpromotable, as a tenured assistant professor. That caused salary and the allied problems that go with academic discontent. He was a quiet and cultured man, with a rueful countenance and raven black hair. He would politely complain to me as a chairman about the inequities, and also state that the immigration people had his birth date wrong, that he was younger by I've forgotten how many years. I didn't realize then that he was staving off retirement, not until he had a heart attack and I visited him in the hospital, when, lo! His hair was pearly white.[2]

But it was under Bob Canzoneri that the program was expanded and formalized.

---

2. Kuhn, "Words in Time," 208–209.

CREATIVE WRITING

Michelle Herman

with the abundant research assistance of undergraduate student workers
Chelsea Hinshaw and Christina Simmons

The birth of the creative writing program at OSU, like so many great revolutions (or wars, for that matter), turns out to be difficult to pin down, but for our purposes we might as well declare its birthday to be when Robert Canzoneri joined the faculty in English. (While it's true that Jonathan Baumbach—who would go on to considerable acclaim as writer of experimental fiction and to co-found the Fiction Collective, which lives on, over four decades later, as Fc2, and continues to publish "artistically adventurous, non-traditional fiction"—taught here from 1961 to 1964, he almost certainly did not teach creative writing courses, and there is no evidence that such courses existed at that time. In any case, Baumbach did not publish his first novel until 1965, after he had decamped for NYU.)

When Bob Canzoneri arrived at Ohio State, Gordon Grigsby had already been teaching here for eleven years, but he had been hired as a specialist in Modern British and American Literature, and his focus did not begin to shift to the writing of poetry until the early seventies, and he did not begin to teach creative writing workshops until later still.

The next significant date in creative writing history is 1971—which marked the hiring of novelist Ernest Lockridge (*Prince Elmo's Fire*), who had been teaching at Yale. Ernest joined the faculty as an untenured Associate Professor (he was tenured the following year), and along with Canzoneri and the instructors Ellin Carter and Janet Overmeyer made up the "creative writing faculty" of the day. The earliest creative writing classes combined poetry and fiction writing, and Ernest remembers the first fiction-writing-only workshops he taught as oversubscribed—with as many as thirty students in each section—and populated, he remembers, with "kids who knew nothing about anything, including, of course, fiction. People self-selected themselves into creative writing classes—most often because it fit their schedules, or because they thought it didn't involve learning anything." (He can recall, however, one undergraduate English major from those early days who "really was" a writer—the short story writer Mary Robison, who would go on to become one of the famous "minimalist" writers of the seventies.) In those days, students entering the M.A. program in English could decide, if they chose, to pursue a "creative writing concentration" and prepare a "creative thesis" rather than a scholarly one. It was not a rigorous process, and creative writing as a discipline was very much a marginalized one. Students of the 1970s recall an "unpleasant environment" in which creative writing was considered the ugly step-child of English studies.

When Ernest arrived on our campus, the Rosalie Rusoff Room (Denney 368) was already up and running: Rosalie Rusoff had been a "senior-program student"—in what is now known as Program 60—of Bob Canzoneri, and after her death in 1969, her husband, a well-known Columbus physician, donated money for the creation of a dedicated creative writing room in her memory. A student from those days, Joan Kotker, remembers the relationship between M.A. students studying literature and those studying creative writing as "hostile." She also recalls the Rusoff Room as a place "where writers could come together to smoke cigarettes."

Another student—in the Ph.D. program—in those days was David Citino, who upon his graduation (in 1974) was hired to teach at OSU Marion. Eleven years later, he would move to the Columbus campus, joining Lockridge, Canzoneri, Grigsby, and prose writer William Allen (*Starkweather*), who had been hired in 1973, as the tenure-track faculty in creative writing. Overmeyer and Carter had by then been joined by another instructor/lecturer, Bob Canzoneri's wife, Candy. David Citino would go on to publish ten collections of poetry and to be named poet laureate of OSU.

On January 12, 1987, Bill Allen sent an "inter-office memo" to Murray Beja, Chair of the Department, following up their "MFA talk the other day." He attached a letter from Vance Bourjaily, who had just launched a new M.F.A. program at Louisiana State, on the model of the Iowa Writers' Workshop, where he had been teaching (and which itself had been established in 1936, the first in the country). Bourjaily offered a thorough accounting of how he had accomplished this herculean task at LSU. Allen also attached an essay by Baxter Hathaway, of Cornell University, in which he passionately argues that M.F.A. will be "the highest degree applicable to academic writing" and compares the degree in stature and meaning for creative writers to the Ph.D. in science and law.

On January 13, Murray responded, confessing to being "intrigued" by both Bourjaily's and Hathaway's ideas and the way they "assume that the MFA is different" from other programs offered by English departments and "fundamentally also assume that that's where the MFA belongs."

And so our M.F.A. program was launched. Slowly. A small mountain of correspondence exists that tracks the invention of our program, including a Five-Year Plan for Creative Writing, a Strategic Planning Process, a hopeful (and unrealistic) budget, and multiple drafts of the proposal that would eventually be brought to the Board of Regents. But first there was a hiring plan, which brought the Department fiction writer Michelle Herman, who was hired expressly to help bring an M.F.A. program to Ohio State. The second step was two additional hires—both in

1989—that brought short story writer Lee K. Abbott (*Dreams of Distant Lives*) and National Poetry Series award winner Kathy Fagan (*The Raft*) aboard. By this time (in fact, just two months before Fagan and Abbott arrived in Columbus), Associate Dean of Humanities Isaac Mowoe wrote a letter of support for the M.F.A. program, addressed to Joan Leitzel, Associate Provost. The letter declared that the M.F.A. degree was "recognized in the profession as the appropriate terminal certification for creative writing" and urged that the Office of Academic Affairs consider the proposal, which (spoiler alert) it did. With the support of Dean G. Micheal Riley and the College of Humanities and the backing of OAA—and after a steady accumulation of inter-office memos and letters, multiple iterations of the plan and proposal, clarifications and counter-clarifications, and ultimately an in-person appearance at the Board of Regents by Professors Abbott, Citino, Fagan, and Herman—eventually (in March 1992) we were granted permission to move forward by the Regents Advisory Committee on Graduate Study. One more inter-office communication, in April 1992 from Murray Beja to "David Citino and the faculty in Creative Writing," closes the loop: "Hey, congratulations about the final, official, definitive, irrevocable word about the MFA. Now what?"

Now What

Professors Abbott, Citino, Fagan, and Herman (for by then Allen was near retirement) agreed to allow M.A. students concentrating in creative writing to request transfer into the new M.F.A. program, as well as to solicit applications for our first class of newly admitted M.F.A. students. In February 1993, the four members of the M.F.A. faculty sat down to create our first M.F.A. admissions list. It included Deborah Way—ranked first in a list of sixteen—who would go on to become Deputy Editor of *O Magazine*.

The very first M.F.A. class earned their degrees in Spring 1993. It consisted of a small number of students to whom we had granted permission to make the transfer. That class included poet and novelist Marcia Douglas (*Notes from a Writer's Book of Cures and Spells*). Poet Erin Belieu (National Poetry Series winner for *Infanta*) was in that "transfer class," too—but she did not stick around to earn her M.F.A. in 1993; she left just short of her degree to earn an M.A. in creative writing at Boston University, published her first book, and taught at Kenyon College (among other institutions) before returning to us to complete her M.F.A. She now directs the M.F.A. program at Florida State University. In 1994 other M.A.-to-M.F.A. transfers graduated with the new degree, including novelist Will Allison (whose books include the *Times* bestseller *Long Drive Home*).

From the start, when the program's founding fathers/mothers began to meet to make plans that went beyond the on-paper proposal, we were committed to creating an M.F.A. program that would fully meet the needs of its (future) students in a way that we had not seen done elsewhere. Unlike the Iowa Writers' Workshop and Columbia University—the two gold standards of the time—we would fully fund all admitted students; we would keep them with us for three years, so that the third year could be spent in intensive thesis work; and we were determined to do all that we could to ensure that any additional faculty hired would be as committed to teaching as they were to their own writing. One aspect of the program that wasn't planned, however, was what we have become, perhaps, most well known for: the mutual support and encouragement among our students and alumni, and the network formed by OSU M.F.A. alumni. Another great and growing strength of our program is its collaborative nature (with Theater, Film Studies, and, increasingly, Art and Dance). Graduate students in other programs not only take our courses but create work in collaboration with our students; students have together created video games (Creative Writing and ACCAD [Advanced Computing Center for the Arts and Design]), graphic narratives (Creative Writing and Art/Painting and Drawing), dance pieces (Creative Writing and Dance), and many other new projects that cross disciplines. Faculty in creative writing frequently serve on thesis committees in other arts areas, and even as faculty and students continue to make their mark in literature—publishing in the highest profile outlets, such as the *New Yorker,* the *Paris Review,* and the *Atlantic Monthly*—we increasingly pursue the creation and exhibition, performance, and publication of new work that crosses over into other disciplines.

Admissions for the M.F.A. program are increasingly selective: each year in fiction, for example, we receive upwards of 150 applications, and we admit just six to eight candidates.

Creative Writing Faculty

David Citino's death in 2005 was a great blow to all of us, both professionally and personally. The poet Andrew Hudgins, whom we had hired in 2001, chaired a search that led to the hiring of another senior poet, Henri Cole, in 2007. Hudgins's retirement in 2016 and Cole's resignation that same year would have left Fagan the lone poet, but the program hired Marcus Jackson (*Neighborhood Register*) in 2016.

Pulitzer Prize finalist Lee Martin (*The Bright Forever*), a fiction and creative nonfiction writer, joined the faculty in 2001, as did fiction writer Erin McGraw (who retired in 2015). Lee Abbott retired in 2012.

Other faculty who have taught in the program over the years include fiction writers Elizabeth Dewberry Vaughn (1992–1996), Lore Segal (1992–1997), and Melanie Rae Thon (1996–2000); and nonfiction writers Bill Roorbach (1995–2001) and Stephen Kuusisto (2000–2007).

The Journal

When Bill Allen was hired, in 1973, it was in part to launch a literary magazine (originally called *The Ohio Journal*, but later changed to *The Journal* to avoid confusion with *The Ohio Review*, housed at Ohio University). The magazine began modestly, as a slender tabloid-sized affair with a crudely rendered cover—and publishing mainly OSU students and faculty, including, for example, Tony Libby, who like Gordon Grigsby before him (and, later, Jeredith Merrin) had made a shift from literary criticism to the writing of poetry—but which would go on to become a nationally recognized, prize-winning journal, now in its fifth decade (making it one of the oldest continuously published literary journals in the nation). David Citino took over its editorship when he came to the Columbus campus in 1985, and in 1990 he passed that torch to Kathy Fagan and Michelle Herman, who acted as co-editors for over two decades. Now the magazine is edited entirely by students in the M.F.A. Program in Creative Writing.

An extremely important hire for another major program in the Department was that of Edward P. J. Corbett in 1966; he came to OSU as a full professor from Creighton University. In those years some 10,000 first-year students took three quarters of "Freshman Composition." As Julian Markels recalls, to get them all into their classes, "on the first day of each quarter, the hundreds of students enrolled in freshman English at a given hour were herded like cattle along a basement corridor, where they were counted out in groups of 26 and led by their teacher to a classroom across campus, who knew where?"[3] The whole program was administered with astounding efficiency and intelligence by Edwin Robbins, but he was not a rhetorician with formal training in the field.

With Corbett, the Department gained an especially renowned scholar of rhetoric. He was the author of numerous books, many of which went into several editions, including *Classical Rhetoric for the Modern Student* (1965), *The Little English Handbook: Choices and Conventions* (1977), *The Elements of Reasoning* (1991), and, co-authored with his former graduate student Robert J. Connors and appearing after Corbett's death in 1998, *Style and Statement* (1999). Connors had already edited *Selected Essays of Edward P. J. Corbett* (1989). A volume in Corbett's honor edited by Connors and two others of Corbett's former students, Lisa S. Ede and Andrea A. Lunsford, was *Essays on Classical Rhetoric and Modern Discourse* (1984), which contained a bibliography of Corbett's writings compiled by his colleague Sara Garnes and another former student, Charles Zarobila.

---

3. Markels, *From Buchenwald*, 80.

FIGURE 5.4. Edward P. J. Corbett

Andrea Lunsford gives us a history of the program he did so much to bring to eminence.

RHETORIC AND COMPOSITION

Andrea Abernethy Lunsford

All historical accountings are in some ways personal, and such is certainly the case with this remembering of rhetoric and composition (now rhetoric, composition, and literacy) at Ohio State University. So first a bit of positioning: some of this remembering is first-hand, from my years as a graduate student (1972–77) and as a faculty member (1986–2000). More of those specific times as the story unfolds.

Since 1960, the Department of English has been located in Denney Hall, named after Joseph Villiers Denney, the rhetorician who served as the first Chair of the Department of Rhetoric (1891–1904) and then as Chair of the Department of Rhetoric and English Literature when the two merged (1904–33).[4] Denney was a well-known progressive educator, colleague and co-author with Michigan's Fred Newton Scott, who was founder and first president of the National Council of

---

4. For a thorough and thoroughly engaging discussion of Denney's work at Ohio State, see Mendenhall, "Joseph V. Denney."

Teachers of English, a group of scholar/teachers who broke away from the Modern Language Association in 1914 to found their own organization. At Ohio State, Denney juggled the competing claims of "practical" versus "liberal" education, arguing for a science of rhetoric that could accommodate both, which he saw as a primary obligation of land grant schools in general and Ohio State in particular. Denney went on to develop a curriculum, beginning with first-year study of The Science of Rhetoric and including additional rhetoric courses such as Advanced Rhetoric, Practical Rhetoric, Advanced Composition, and Analysis of Prose. In composition courses, students were invited to write in their areas of interest, one course focusing on writing in the College of Arts, Philosophy, and Science (of which Denney served as Dean from 1901 to 1921) and another on writing in the College of Engineering. Eventually, Denney led the way in developing a graduate program as well: Rhetorical Theory and Criticism for M.A. students was offered in 1901, and other courses, such as History of Rhetoric and Development of Rhetorical Ideas, followed.

When the Department of Rhetoric and the Department of English Literature merged in 1904,[5] Denney was a prime mover, writing to President William Oxley Thompson that bringing the two departments together would delete redundancies and overlaps and be beneficial to the University and its students. And Denney chaired this merged Department as well, establishing it as a unit devoted to the study of the English language, English and American literature, and composition, which Nancy Dasher described in her 1970 history of the Department as including "principles of Rhetoric, practice in written Narrative Description, Exposition, Brief-making, and Argumentation."[6] While composition courses were to focus on the immediate and practical needs of students, rhetoric underlay these classes. As Dasher put it, "Mr. Denney was a rhetoric man at heart."[7]

This "rhetoric man" had a lasting impact on the Department (as well as the University), and his legacy can be seen in later decades in the ongoing emphasis on history of the language, on practical criticism, and on college composition. While some historians have argued that rhetoric deteriorated into what I. A. Richards in 1936 called the "dreariest and least profitable part of the waste that the unfortunate travel through in Freshman English"[8] and thus led to the marginalization of the field, the case at Ohio State seems much more complicated than that, especially given Denney's insistence that rhetoric encompass academic *and* professional discourses and that students must always write with purpose and

---

5. This "merger" was more properly a "re-merger," since before Denney arrived at Ohio State in 1891 there had been a Department of English Language and Literature.

6. Dasher, *Brief History,* 29–30.

7. Dasher, *Brief History,* 33.

8. Richards, *Philosophy of Rhetoric,* 3.

audience firmly in mind. Indeed, in an 1897 essay, he insisted that thought could not be divided from form: "even questions of punctuation" demanded attention to both.

Nevertheless, rhetoric's role in the Department slipped considerably, especially after Denney's retirement in 1933, although courses in composition continued to hold a place in the curriculum, especially the first-year composition course and the more advanced writing course designed for engineering students. (So entrenched was this particular course that when it was dropped during the 1980s in a time of severe budget cuts as a "service" the Department could no longer afford to provide to the College of Engineering, the outrage of that group was loud and long-lived.) The first-year program went along steadily, perhaps more out of habit than anything else, headed up by Ed Robbins from 1954 to 1966. With the hiring of Edward P. J. Corbett in 1966 to direct the Writing Program, however, the Department gained another "rhetoric man," though he did not immediately revive other rhetoric courses.

Stories of Ed Corbett's tenure as Director of First-Year Writing are legion. A very early riser, he was reputed to arrive in Denney Hall well before 8:00 and stride up and down the halls, looking for any instructors/TAs who might be arriving late. He also gave a quiz in the opening minute or two of his classes, and woe be to those who arrived late: they received a zero for that quiz. But Corbett's ebullience, droll wit, and flair for the dramatic endeared him to many, and as he would have said, he "carried on in the finest traditions" as Director until 1971. Professor Don Good, a specialist in nineteenth-century literature, took over directing first-year writing from 1971 to 1974 and then the job fell to Margaret (Peg) Blickle, who rose from part-time instructor in English and Speech in 1945 to Associate Professor, with an interest in technical writing, drama, and puppetry (!), and directed the program for the 1974–75 year. In 1975, however, the Department hired a "rhetoric woman," Susan Passler Miller, who swept into the job with enormous energy, intellect, and—almost immediately—controversy that surrounded her for the three years of her tenure. Miller brought with her the excitement of the "new" composition studies, restructuring the first-year writing curriculum to focus on process and bringing in young scholars like Rick Coe, Erika Lindemann, David Bartholomae, and Mina Shaughnessy, all of whose work focused squarely on student writing, to give talks to the growing number of graduate students interested in this field of study. In addition, based on contemporary research on Ohio State student writers, she launched—with the help of Sara Garnes and Suellynn Duffey—Ohio State's highly respected Basic Writing Workshop. This basic writing program succeeded in shedding the "remedial" label, allowing Workshop students to gain college credit for the work they did there, and showing that these writers had significant writing strengths as well as weaknesses. Under Duffey's directorship—and later that of Mindy Wright—the Workshop helped generations of first-year students persist in the University.

Frank O'Hare arrived in 1978, continuing the trend of hiring rhetoric and composition scholars to direct the first-year program; his work on sentence combining was influential, inspiring additional work among graduate students. Sara Garnes joined the faculty that same year, inaugurating a decade of hiring in the field: Ron Fortune, Ann Dobyns, Terrence Odlin, Kitty Locker, H. Lewis Ulman, Beverly Moss, Nan Johnson, Keith Walters, Roger Cherry, Kay Halasek, Brenda Brueggemann, and Marcia Dickson joined during that decade, and I returned to Ohio State as Professor in 1986. By the time Jacqueline Jones Royster joined the faculty in 1992, the rhetoric and composition group was well established, developing courses at both the undergraduate and graduate levels and advocating for student writers and student writing as well as for detailed attention to the history and theory of rhetoric. In addition, this group spearheaded the development of the Center for the Study and Teaching of Writing, the proposal for which was developed in 1997. I served as its first Director and was followed by Beverly Moss and, most recently, by Dickie Selfe.

Today, some of those scholars have moved on (Keith Walters, Brenda Brueggemann, Ann Dobyns, Jackie Royster) or retired (Louie Ulman, Terry Odlin, Marcia Dickson), and the Department mourned the 2005 passing of Kitty Locker, who had done so much to develop business and technical writing and to inspire a generation of graduate students to conduct research in that area. But others arrived, including Susan Delagrange, Scott DeWitt, James Fredal, Wendy Hesford, Harvey Graff, Cynthia Selfe, Richard/Dickie Selfe, and Christa Teston. Now called the program in Rhetoric, Composition, and Literacy, this vibrant group offers a popular undergraduate minor in writing and teaches courses from first-year writing to digital media studies and transnational rhetorics, to graduate seminars in these and many other areas of the field, including technical and business writing, gender studies, history and theory of rhetoric, women's rhetorics, literacy theory, community service writing, and more. If Joseph Villiers Denney was the Department's first "rhetoric man," then today's faculty includes *many* rhetoric men and women, though the looming retirement of Cindy and Dickie Selfe in a time of limited hiring suggests a need for additional recruitment at the senior level.

But these last paragraphs give only the briefest sketch of the development of the field of rhetoric, composition, and literacy studies within the Department. To get a deeper sense of that history, let's turn back to the early 1970s, a time of huge national turmoil but also of great intellectual excitement. When I arrived at Ohio State in the fall of 1972 (the admissions committee had put me on the wait list, but had eventually gotten down to me, so I was finally accepted), Ohio and the nation were only two years away from the Kent State killing of students protesting

Nixon's expansion of the Vietnam War; sentiment against the war was at a fever pitch, and Vietnam vets were beginning to show up in college classrooms, including those at Ohio State. The spirit of the sixties was also still alive and well in Columbus, where resistance to institutional authority led to a growing movement to open college and university doors to students who had been left out for too long. While Ohio State did not have an "open admissions" movement as they did at CUNY, we were certainly affected by its ambition and reach.

Those years in the early seventies were pretty free-wheeling, and I remember waves of cigarette (and pot) smoke wafting down the halls and in classrooms of the time. While I came to Ohio State because I had read Ed Corbett's *Classical Rhetoric for the Modern Student* and wanted to learn about the field of rhetoric and composition, when I arrived I found that Ed was teaching eighteenth-century lit and The Bible as literature—much to my chagrin. But he was also editing *College Composition and Communication,* and I had the enormous good fortune— thanks to Dan Barnes, who taught my very first graduate seminar and who took me down to meet "Mr. Corbett"—to serve as his Assistant Editor. Thus began my education in the field: every week or two I would go into Ed's office for an independent study on the history of rhetoric, starting with Socrates and going up to Kenneth Burke. Ed was infinitely patient, greeting me (always) as "Big Old Andrea"—pronounced An-DRAY-ah—and always sending me off with a clap on the back and a "This is what we've been training for." As I read every submission to the journal, I had a crash course on composition studies too, and through Ed I learned of James Golden and Goodwin Berquist, rhetoricians in the Speech and Communication Department from whom I audited a series of courses on the history and theory of rhetoric.

Ed Corbett taught, mentored, and inspired a whole generation of student scholars. His scholarly work was always meticulously researched and beautifully written: he was a stickler for style and rhetorical flourishes/word play. Readers can get a sense of Ed's range in Bob Connors's edited volume *Selected Essays of Edward P. J. Corbett* (1989). When Ed died a decade later (June 24, 1998) at 78, tributes and remembrances poured in: a number of them were published in *Rhetoric Review.* In that issue, Connors wrote:

> He was one of the few remaining members of that group of teachers and scholars who created the discipline of composition studies in the 1960s, a rare scholar and brilliant expositor of classical rhetoric whose works made it available to many of us. Those who knew him also knew he was a humble and lovable man who taught more by the example of his generosity and humanity than by his writing and scholarship. As editor of *CCC* from 1973 to 1979, he helped many of us get started in publishing. He was my graduate

director and mentor, and I was proud to say he was my co-author and friend. We shall not see his like again.[9]

Corbett's work at Ohio State to restore rhetoric was echoed across the country—James Kinneavy at Texas, Jix Lloyd Jones at Iowa, Richard Lanham at UCLA, Ross Winterowd at USC—all were working to bring rhetoric back to English Department consciousness, and thus helping departments prepare for the massive changes, especially in technology, that were facing students and faculty alike. And in the early seventies, Geneva Smitherman (who began in Harvard's Afro-American Studies) began publishing work that, along with that of Mina Shaughnessy, focused attention on the fact that "the student writer" was not always white or male or middle class, and influenced generations of scholars to enrich our understanding of the rich diversity of our student bodies.

During those years, I was not alone in my interest in studying rhetoric and composition. The Department was not admitting students to study this field, but as the seventies wore on, some students of literature became interested in the field and began to shift their foci, all of them welcomed and mentored by Corbett. Slowly, students who had been specializing in literary topics also began to take an interest in this relatively new field. But many more, faced with a very poor job market, found that their association with Ed Corbett and rhetoric allowed them to shift focus. Lisa Ede, who graduated in 1975 with a dissertation on Lewis Carroll and other "nonsense" writers, landed her first academic job at SUNY Brockport—as director of writing—and went on to develop and direct Oregon State's Center for Writing and Learning for decades. John Ruszkiewicz, a Renaissance scholar in grad school, went to Texas, where he directed the writing program in English and went on to found the current Department of Writing and Rhetoric. Elizabeth Flynn, a modernist and feminist, focused on gender and writing and built a distinguished career in rhetoric and composition at Michigan Tech. As the number of "switchovers" grew (and I think here of others like Carmen Schmersahl, Gerald Mulderig, Mary Rosner, and Betsy Brown), the Department began allowing students to take general examinations in the field (I believe I was the first one to do so, in 1975) and, slowly but surely, to admit students who wanted to specialize in rhetoric and composition. And, of course, these students began to write dissertations in the field, as I did on basic writing.

These incipient changes, and the urging of graduate students, led Ed Corbett to develop some graduate seminars in the field. By the time I graduated in 1977, he was teaching a graduate seminar on style as well as one on rhetorical history. He went on to teach two legendary NEH Seminars on rhetorical topics, the first of

9. Connors, "Memoriam," 126.

which included Sharon Crowley, and the second James Porter. Ed later said that his graduate students and NEH "seminarians" taught him as much as he taught them, and in the years to come he acknowledged—with grace and wit—the limitations of his presentation of rhetorical history, which reflected the tradition as western, white, and male. Seminarians like Crowley (who directed writing programs at Texas and Arizona State before her recent retirement) and later students like Cheryl Glenn (currently the Liberal Arts Research Professor of English and Women's Studies at Penn State and former Chair of the Conference on College Composition and Communication) did a great deal to broaden this view of rhetorical history, always with Ed's support and praise.

The years from the mid-eighties to Ed's death in 1998 saw development of rhetoric, writing, and literacy studies as the faculty group struggled to establish respect—and a solid footing—in a department dominated by the study of literature. In the ensuing years that struggle has continued, but the rhetoric and composition faculty has had the benefit of being part of a large, omnibus department that includes not only rhetoric but also folklore, applied linguistics, performance studies, creative writing, and more. In any case, the rhetoric and composition group has attracted many outstanding graduate students who have gone on to bring change to the departments they joined and to make significant contributions to higher education in general as well as to our field of study. In addition to those already mentioned, I think of Esther Rauch (now retired but formerly Vice President of the Bangor Theological Seminary), Krista Ratcliff (former president of the Rhetoric Society of America and currently Chair of the Department at Purdue), Roxanne Mountford (who founded the Department of Rhetoric and Writing at Kentucky and is now distinguished Professor at Oklahoma), Kermit Campbell (early researcher on Black vernacular and now Chair of the Department of Rhetoric and Writing at Colgate); Amy Goodburn (currently Associate Vice Chancellor at the University of Nebraska); Carrie Leverenz (Director of the Institute for Critical and Creative Expression at Texas Christian); Jaime Mejia (Associate Professor of English at Texas State who has mentored an entire generation of Chicano/a students); Sarah Sloane (Professor of English, Colorado State); Roger and Heather Graves (now Professors at U. Alberta, who have led the way in establishing writing curricula across Canada); Jerry Nelms (Director of Developmental Writing at Wright State); Bob Yagelski (Director of Writing and Critical Inquiry at SUNY Albany); Pat Sullivan (Director of the Program in Writing and Rhetoric at the University of Colorado); Carole Papper (Director of the University Writing Program at Ball State and recently retired from Hofstra); Pamela Martin (Executive Vice President at Voorhees College and former President of Allen University). I could go on. But let me simply add that in addition to the administrative roles these graduates have held, they have published scores and scores of books and articles making significant and ongoing contributions to the field of rhetoric, writing, and literacy. In doing so, they have carried with them the experience and knowledge—and the ethos of care—they gained as members of the Ohio State Department of English.

I consider myself infinitely fortunate to be in their company. As Ed Corbett probably would say, in his occasional dip into French, "quel colleagues!" Rhetoric women and men carrying on the traditions established by Joseph Villiers Denney, Ed Corbett, and so many others.

Also hired in 1966 was James R. Kincaid, as a Victorianist. He went on to prominence in that field as well as in a number of areas of cultural studies. His publications include *Dickens and the Rhetoric of Laughter* (1972); *Tennyson's Major Poems* (1975); *Novels of Anthony Trollope* (1977); *Child-Loving: The Erotic Child and Victorian Culture* (1992); and *Erotic Innocence: The Culture of Child Molesting* (1998), as well as several novels, including *Lost* (2012). He left Ohio State in 1977 to become Chair of English at the University of Colorado and went on to become the Aerol Arnold Professor of English at the University of Southern California, and then, in retirement from USC, Adjunct Professor at the University of Pittsburgh. He had received OSU's Alumni Award for Distinguished Teaching in 1973. He was a major presence while in the Department and has remained its loyal friend since. He and Al Kuhn co-edited *Victorian Literature and Society: Essays Presented to Richard D. Altick* (1984).

Rolf Soellner came to the Department in 1967 as a Professor and remained until his retirement in 1987. He published two volumes with the OSU Press, *Shakespeare's Patterns of Self-Knowledge* (1972) and *Timon of Athens, Shakespeare's Pessimistic Tragedy* (1979). A native of Germany, he had expanded his knowledge of English and his love of English literature while a prisoner of war during World War II.

Anthony Libby was also hired in 1967, as an Assistant Professor. He retired as a Professor in 2003. Having published *Mythologies of Nothing: Mystical Death in American Poetry, 1940–70*, he turned especially to writing his own poetry; *The Secret Turning of the Earth* was published by Kent State University Press in 1995. Libby also took up photography; he had contributed significantly to the Department's teaching of film.

Another Assistant Professor hired in 1967 was John Sena, whose field was the eighteenth century. He was promoted to Associate Professor in 1970 and to full Professor in 1988. He published *A Bibliography of Melancholy, 1660–1800* in 1970 and *The Best-Natured Man: Sir Samuel Garth, Physician and Poet* in

FIGURE 5.5. John Sena

1986. He had the distinction of receiving the University Alumni Award for Distinguished Teaching twice, in 1975 and 1985. Always interested in business as well as literary scholarship, with Stephen Strasser he also wrote *Work Is Not a Four-Letter Word: Improving the Quality of Your Work Life* (1992) and *From Campus to Corporation* (1993). He taught a number of courses for the Division of Health Services at OSU, and after his retirement in 2000, he had a second career running motivational seminars in that field throughout the US and abroad.

In 1968, Mildred Brand Munday was promoted from Instructor to tenured Assistant Professor; she was to have an important role in the development of Women's Studies in the Department and the University. (See the account of "Women's and Gender Studies" by Valerie Lee in chapter 8.)

Also in 1968, W. J. Thomas Mitchell came to OSU. He was promoted to Associate Professor in 1974. *Blake's Composite Art: A Study of the Illuminated Poetry* appeared in 1978, the same year he moved to the University of Chicago. Tom continued his scholarship and criticism on visual culture with *The Language of Images* (1980) and several other books. He became the Gaylord Donnelley Distinguished Service Professor of English and Art History at Chicago, and the editor of *Critical Inquiry*.

Two other appointments important to the life of the University were made that year: those of the medievalist Christian Zacher and the Renaissance scholar David Frantz.

Zacher (promoted to Associate Professor in 1974 and to full Professor in 1986) published *Curiosity and Pilgrimage: The Literature of Discovery in Fourteenth-Century England* in 1976. He and Donald Howard had co-edited *Critical Studies of Sir Gawain and the Green Knight* in 1968, and in 1992 he co-edited *The Idea of Medieval Literature: New Essays on Chaucer and Medieval Culture in Honor of Donald R. Howard*. He was also one of the general editors of *The American Midwest: An Interpretive Encyclopedia* (2007). He wrote the volume on the presidency of Karen Holbrook for the series of institutional histories of the University: *The Holbrook Years: 2002–2007* (2012). For a number of years, he anonymously produced fake weekly Departmental newsletters, with imagined "news" or bibliographic entries featuring at one time or another just about all his colleagues.

Frantz was promoted to Associate Professor in 1975 and to Professor in 1991. He published *Festum Voluptatis: A Study of Renaissance Erotica* in 1989. He had received the University Alumni Award for Distinguished Teaching in 1976. He served as Vice Chair of the Department under both Julian Markels and Morris Beja, and then went on to a distinguished career in the University at large.

In fact, both Zacher and Frantz, who as scholars and teachers have variously interacted with one another because of their adjacent fields of study, have served the University in significant administrative positions, and both have received the University Faculty Award for Distinguished University Service.

Zacher directed the Center for Medieval and Renaissance Studies (as have other English Department colleagues, Nicholas Howe and Richard Green); he was Associate Dean of the College of Humanities, co-created and directed the Humanities Institute, and was secretary of the University Senate.

Frantz has been both the Associate Dean and Acting Dean of the College of Humanities; he was especially visible within the central administration as Secretary of the Board of Trustees.

In these and other ways these two colleagues have helped to influence the shape of Ohio State, together with the many others from the English Department who have had important posts outside the Department—including, within the scope of this history of the Department to the year 2000, Mark Auburn, Joseph Denney, Steven Fink, James Fullington, John Gabel, Don Good, Richard Green, Kay Halasek, Harlan Hatcher, Nicholas Howe, Stanley Kahrl, Sebastian Knowles, Al Kuhn, Valerie Lee, Anthony Libby, Marlene Lon-

FIGURE 5.6. Christian K. Zacher

FIGURE 5.7. David O. Frantz

genecker, Beverly Moss, John Muste, John Roberts, Jacqueline Jones Royster, John Sena, Amy Shuman, and Susan Williams.

Within the Department, David Frantz was also an important presence in the realm of sports and athletics, which played a role that belies easy but false stereotypes about "English professors"—and English majors and graduate students.

SPORTS IN THE DEPARTMENT OF ENGLISH— AS REMEMBERED BY DAVID FRANTZ AND JULIAN MARKELS

David Frantz

In writing these paragraphs, I have made no attempt at "accuracy"; rather, these are really memories of the place of sports in the English Department going back to my first year in the Department, 1968. It has not been possible to check some dates, although that would provide a more definitive timeline on such matters (for example the date of the last Jock Banquet).

From my first quarter at Ohio State I was made aware (although how I do not exactly know) that there was a culture of participation in OSU's vast intramural sports program by the Department of English. I was invited to play in some weekend pickup touch football games; the participants, mostly all male graduate students, were the remnants of a touch football team that had competed in the past in the intramural program of the University. They were known as Kuhn's Krushers (after then chair Al Kuhn, who might recently have just finished a term as Chair of the University's Athletic Council—the only University committee to which people vied for appointment, carrying with it as a benefit a free bowl trip).

That winter (1969) there was an active intramural basketball team, again mostly populated by graduate students, but now including some of the new faculty, including yours truly and Tom Mitchell. A mainstay on that team was Paul De Muro, a married graduate student originally from Philadelphia, who hosted that winter what apparently was already a strong tradition, the Jock Banquet. This was a social affair that included a potluck dinner, a speaker (Fran Utley my first year), and much drinking and dancing. It was at this event that first year that I became aware of a number of affairs involving faculty and graduate students. The Jock Banquet grew over the years that I recall to include an annual award—the False Florimell Golden Jock Award (Books III and IV of Spenser's *Faerie Queene*, for those of you wondering) that went to the best male or female athlete in the Department. This "trophy" had been created out of a gilded jock strap on a stand that for some time sat in the office of Mike Rupright when he was the Administrative Assistant of the English Department Chair. As I recall, the final Jock Banquet was held at the home of graduate students Ed Yasuna and Andrea Gilchrist. This festive event featured a vocal performance by Bill Allen's then wife, who sang "I have a lovely shuttlecock" to great approval. The speaker at that banquet was John Muste, who had played basketball at Brown University with Joe Paterno.

The arrival of Jim Phelan as a faculty member transformed the English Department basketball team from one that enjoyed lunchtime participation in pick-up games in the Green Gym in the old Larkins Hall (since replaced by the palatial RPAC), along with Saturday rental of a gym at rec centers, to a team that competed university-wide in the intramurals. Soon after Jim arrived, a graduate student, Will Miles, also joined the Department. Jim, at 6'4", having played at Boston College, and Will, at least 6'6", having played at Capital University, gave the English Department two real basketball players. They were so good that our team, now known as Ezra's Pounders, could compete favorably in the intramural faculty-staff league. Other participants on those teams were faculty members Pat Mullen, Rick Finholt, Mac Davis, and David Schwalm, and a number of graduate students, most notably R. J. Collins and Jack Shortlidge. A tradition after games was to repair to Larry's, a bar on High Street, for beers and stories. The highlight for the Pounders was a championship game against the Phys Ed department in which the English Department emerged victorious, defeating a team led by Bob Huggins, later the coach at the University of Cincinnati and now at West Virginia, who was at the time a graduate student at OSU. There was at one time a university-wide basketball tournament sponsored by a Black fraternity in which an expanded Ezra's Pounders, with some outside ringers replacing those of us who were mediocre players at best, had some considerable success, beating a team made up of OSU football players ("Cooper's Slow White Guys") on its way to the championship game.

Three other sports figured in the culture of the Department: softball, volleyball, and poker. I believe there was an intramural softball team for some time, but the annual highlight of that sport was the game between the faculty and students (mostly graduate, but I think some undergraduates participated as well) that was a ritual at the Spring picnic. Many faculty participated in this co-ed event. Among the stalwarts for the faculty were Jim Phelan, Jim Battersby, David Citino, Robbie Kantor, Lisa Kiser, Robin Bell Markels, Mac Davis, Steve Fink, Chris Zacher, and many others. It hardly need be said that the faculty completely dominated this event year after year.[10]

---

10. Martin Beller, a former graduate student, writes in an email to the authors of this history (July 15, 2015): "Many of my liveliest memories are focused on The Grendels—the English Graduate Department's intramural softball team. We played football among ourselves much of the fall and winter (Saturday mornings at 9:00, hung over or not), but the softball team played in an intramural league, and we won half or more of our games, usually made the playoffs, and occasionally advanced a round or two. I was known as 'Marty the Magnificent,' with deep, cutting irony, but I was still the starting 2nd baseman. The right fielder was even worse than I was."

Julian Markels

We had a softball team called the Woolf Pack that also won the University intramurals, maybe in the late seventies into the early eighties. Regular team members included Bob Collins, Jim Battersby, Lisa Kiser, Mac Davis, Chris Zacher, Robin Bell, Pat Mullen, Betsy Brown (grad student), and her husband Homer (the Joe DiMaggio of the team). The softball team was by then a tradition that went back to the sixties; I can remember Henry St. Onge, a grad student who defied Novice Fawcett's Speakers Rule by inviting a radical to speak in his backyard, as a terrific shortstop in our departmental games in the sixties.

There was also for some years (also in the seventies as I remember) a Departmental Sunday volleyball game—which began in French Fieldhouse and then migrated to outdoor venues in the summer and to a Jesse Owens Quonset hut in the winter. Bob Canzoneri and Candy Barnes, Robin Bell and I (that's where we met), Dave Carpenter (grad student), and Ford Swetnam were regulars.

And here are two precious sports memories of mine. I was Chair when our Phelan-led basketball defeated the OSU football team in the University-wide tournament, and several times during the ensuing weeks I was accosted on the Oval by acquaintances who needled me for recruiting basketball players instead of scholars in the English Department. Also, most of the players on those basketball teams, and also our softball teams, were a decade older than their opponents (at the very least). Some had ace bandages on their knees or elbows, and they all looked gimpy one way or another, but most of them understood and loved the sport they were playing and made up in mental focus and intensity for their physical limitations. They won most of their games.

In a perhaps related story, Al Kuhn remembers, in his "Words in Time: Essays and Occasions," how Woody Hayes came to see him one day about Mike Ingram, a linebacker who had had trouble passing what was then called the Freshman Remedial English program:

"Dr. Kuhn," he said, "I know Mike has problems. I have tried to tutor him myself. He works hard at English. I have seen him twist and sweat over his compositions. I know that the pencil isn't comfortable in his hand, but dog-gone [a favorite expression], he works hard." (The coach had an intense and personal pleading in his voice and face, as he leaned across my desk.) "Don't you think he's worth at least a D?"

I am not generally quick witted, but a coachlike answer came to mind. Said I, "Coach whom do you put in the backfield on Saturday afternoon?

Those who try or those who produce?" He glared first, then his eye twinkled, and he laughed. "You got me there," he said, and he left.[11]

And while we're at it, we might as well mention here the Department's traditional poker game, which has been in existence at least since the 1950s, though perhaps long before that. In any case, regular players since the 1960s have included, in more or less chronological order, John Muste, John Gabel, Hugh Atkinson (head of the Libraries), David Frantz, Chris Zacher (and, often, his son Sam), Tom Cooley, Stan Kahrl, John Sena, Murray Beja, Lee Abbott, Seb Knowles, Sam Choi, and Steve Kern (of the History Department). Usually there have been six or seven players. Games are held every couple of months, at the home of whoever calls it. As that list indicates, players have almost always (though not quite always) been men. Betting is very modest; it's been a nickel and dime game for decades. Most of the games played would be familiar to any poker player, but some are, well, eccentric. We have already mentioned, in chapter 4, the "particularly grueling game with complicated and hard-to-master rules" called Alyce Moore, a card-passing game in which a participant can be forced to ruin a good hand, "just as," one senior faculty remembers, "the Chair's assistant could better or worsen one's position in the game of Department life."

The year 1968 was of course a momentous one in the entire nation, with tensions in regard to civil rights, protests against the war in Vietnam and at the Democratic convention in Chicago, and the assassinations of Martin Luther King Jr., and Robert F. Kennedy. The OSU English Department was not immune to the turmoil. One example—which began with what seemed at first a totally minor issue—brings us back to Matt Bruccoli. In those years the Department put out a dittoed newsletter each week, edited by a faculty member. The editor in 1968 was William A. Gibson, an Assistant Professor who had been hired as an eighteenth-century scholar in 1964 (he was promoted to Associate in 1970 and left the next year for Idaho State and then the University of Minnesota Duluth). Gibson placed an item in the newsletter one week announcing an upcoming meeting for those interested in the candidacy for President of Eugene McCarthy. Bruccoli, who was deeply conservative, objected and demanded that Gibson be fired. Al Kuhn appointed what has to be considered a blue-ribbon committee of Fran Utley and John Muste to make a recommendation to the Department. It recommended that in the future no political announcements be included in the newsletter, but

11. Kuhn, "Words in Time," 203.

of course also concluded that Gibson should not be admonished or punished. When the full Department met on the matter, Bruccoli vociferously argued that Gibson should be fired; when the Department overwhelmingly voted not to agree, he stormed out of the room in a fury, immediately turning back to say that he had intended to resign if he lost, but that instead he would stay in the Department and fight.

But then he did give Kuhn a letter of resignation. Al went to Bruccoli's home that evening and persuaded him not to follow through on that—which meant that Bruccoli stayed in the Department one more year, during which he refused to speak to anyone, with only an exception or two. One was Daniel Barnes, who was hired that next year (see below). Poor Dan—who had felt gratitude toward Bruccoli for a previous professional favor—found himself glommed on to, forbidden as it were from being friendly to anyone else while Bruccoli was around. (One day, for example, several colleagues were walking from the Faculty Club and, on the Oval, passed Barnes walking with Bruccoli, who as usual did not return their greeting; but when they turned back after they all passed each other, they saw Barnes with his hand behind his back wiggling his fingers.) It was a very awkward year. Bruccoli then left for the University of South Carolina, where he went on to an extremely prominent career.[12]

Another controversy, a non-political one, loomed over the Department around that time. Kuhn asked the senior staff to agree that a number of the Instructors—who had no tenure—be let go, and that the remaining ones be awarded tenure as Assistant Professors. The faculty agreed, but one of those not being retained was Brenda Wilson, the daughter of John Harold Wilson, who was bitter about the decision.

Daniel Barnes came to the Department in 1968. He was the author of many essays in American literature and Folklore. He was promoted to Associate Professor in 1973. A wonderfully skilled piano player, his talents were in demand at parties and other social events; when he retired in 1998, he pursued a second career as a pianist, especially in Coshocton, to which he and his wife,

---

12. Some years later, Murray Beja was at an MLA conference in New York, and early in the morning he was in the almost empty lobby of the Hilton Hotel, with Bruccoli walking toward him. Beja reached out his hand, and Bruccoli reflexively shook it. Beja told Bruccoli he was glad that after so much time he was willing to shake his hand. Then realizing who he was, Bruccoli slapped Beja's hand away and snapped, "Why shouldn't I shake your hand, you son of a bitch. You were all a bunch of lily-livered cowards. And not only that, you were one of the leaders!" (Beja regrettably denies that he had been.) That evening, Joe Katz—who had been a friend of Bruccoli, and like him interested in textual studies, and who had followed him to South Carolina—came to the English Department party to socialize with former colleagues. He and Beja were chatting when Katz suddenly said, "Did you hear the latest about Matt? In the lobby this morning he took a swing at a guy!"

FIGURE 5.8. Daniel Barnes

Holly Downing, moved. Eventually, as illness forced Barnes to give up that livelihood, they came back to Columbus. Dan died in 2016. For more on his scholarship, see the account by Patrick Mullen and Amy Shuman of the role of Folklore within the Department, below.

Carl Marshall, who had received his M.A. at OSU in 1947 and his Ph.D. in 1954 with a dissertation on William Dean Howells, became the Department's first African American full Professor in 1969, at the Lima Campus. Two years later he moved to the Columbus campus. He retired in 1972.

In the late sixties the University attempted to respond to a long series of protests, especially by African American students, calling for more openness to their needs and demands. For example, in April 1968 over four hundred African American students locked themselves in the Administration Building—now Bricker Hall—and presented the University administration with their demands, notably for more black faculty and students.

In 1968 a committee was created to look into the question of creating a Black Studies Department. Presumably because he had proposed the first course in African American literature, and had published a bit in the field, Morris Beja was appointed to the committee and became its chair. Simultaneously, and obviously assuming the committee's recommendation would be favorable, the University also appointed a committee to recommend the first Department

Chair; that committee was chaired by John Muste. The "Afro-American Studies Committee," consisting of both faculty and students, faced a number of difficulties in its deliberations—and at the end in finding a home for what became the Division (not yet the Department) of Black Studies. Several deans rejected the idea immediately as too controversial, but Charles Babcock, the Dean of the College of Humanities, was welcoming, and that is where the Division was housed, in 1969. For the role of African American Studies within the Department of English, see Valerie Lee's account in chapter 8 of the present history.

Of course, there were other causes of student unrest in the late sixties and early seventies—centering above all on the Vietnam War. Ohio State was not unique—anything but. According to the report of the "Committee on Inquiry" on "The Spring Events at Ohio State," presented to Faculty Council in November of 1970, "In the first six months of 1969, 292 major student protests on 232 university campuses closed two dozen schools. By the late Spring of 1970, there were large-scale demonstrations on at least 760 campuses—or one-third of the total in this country—and on virtually all university campuses."[13]

Ironically, it was the centennial year of OSU—1970—that became the most troubled in its entire history. Campus disruptions occurred at Ohio State on and off throughout April (and sporadically before and after that). Strikes were called, and picket lines set up at various buildings near the Oval, including Denney Hall, the first floor of which students at times occupied.[14] On April 29, some of the confrontations became violent, and everyone in Denney Hall was told to leave; the violence continued for a couple of days, with the National Guard now present on campus. Tear gas tossed by the Guard on April 30 affected both strikers and bystanders. There was a widespread feeling that vacillation and indecision on the part of the central administration only made things worse. The confrontations ultimately led President Fawcett to declare on May 6 that the University would close the next day, and that students, faculty, and staff had to leave campus.

The English Department met on May 1 for a meeting of several hours. According to the Committee of Inquiry, the Department passed a series of resolutions:

---

13. Committee of Inquiry, "Spring Events," 7. The Committee of Inquiry consisted of eight faculty members, including Robert Canzoneri of the English Department, and one undergraduate and one graduate student, all male. It was chaired by Louis Nemzer of the Department of Political Science.

14. Dick Martin remembers how Ruth Hughey and John Muste had to maneuver their crutches through piles of students' bodies on the floor of Denney Hall as they left the building.

FIGURE 5.9. Student picket line in front of Denney Hall, Spring 1970

These pointed to the conditions on campus—the continuing strike, the atmosphere of possible violence and reaction to that violence, the threat of either vocal or physical disruption of classes—and expressed support to any teacher "who finds it impossible to meet normally scheduled classes." They also recognized the right of students to exercise their conscience in deciding on their class attendance, but declared it "is the teacher's responsibility to tell his students what he expects of them." The Department offered to give extra time to students desiring tutoring or make-up work if they could not go to class. The resolutions also urged the University administration to request the immediate withdrawal of police from the campus, and the removal of the National Guard as soon as possible. The essential core of the English Department's recommendations was contained in the following resolution:

> Under strike conditions prevailing around many classroom build-
> ings since Wednesday, April 29, we have not been able to conduct
> normal classes and properly teach our subject. It is time for the Uni-
> versity administration to support the faculty by negotiating seriously
> with the striking students. . . . We urge the University administra-
> tion to recognize that the striking students, like all other students,

are not clients of the University, but members of it, and to negotiate immediately the issues that caused the strike.[15]

There was a widespread feeling that, facing profoundly challenging problems, Al Kuhn, as Charles Wheeler put it, "handled the difficult situation with great skill" ("O. S. U.," page 4).

The decision by President Nixon to send American troops into Cambodia on May 1, and above all the horror of the killings by members of the National Guard of four students at Kent State on May 4, made the atmosphere all the more explosive. Attempts to ease tensions and prevent violence often centered on the role of the Green Ribbon Commission, which had originated in 1964 but now came into its own. The Commission consisted of volunteer faculty wearing the eponymous green ribbon around their sleeves, who tried to intervene in or mediate confrontations between the students and the authorities—the administration, campus security, the National Guard, sometimes other faculty—without themselves taking sides. The coordinator for the English Department was Mildred Munday, and Wally Maurer was the campus-wide Chair of the Commission and in the forefront of its creation and activities. According to William J. Shkurti in his valuable *The Ohio State University in the Sixties*, "The faculty members who participated in the Green Ribbon Commission deserve special recognition for their efforts. One student called them the 'real heroes' of the spring's events."[16] Yet some people regarded those wearing the green ribbon as having been co-opted, as somehow selling out to, or serving the needs of, the powers that be.[17] But Shkurti also reports that "Political

15. Committee of Inquiry, "Spring Events," 85–86. This report says the meeting occurred May 4. In his "The O. S. U. Campus Disorders," Charles Wheeler dates it May 1; he cites the Committee report but says, "I am inclined to believe my own chronology" (p. 4 of unnumbered pages), which was written during or very soon after the events it records. Morris Beja, who was at the meeting, believes that Wheeler is correct, and that it is highly unlikely that the meeting occurred on the date of the Kent State killings. He believes that a dittoed memo quoted in the Committee report, a copy of which is in his possession, and which is dated May 4, is a report on the meeting to the Department and does not indicate the date of the meeting itself.

16. Shkurti, *Ohio State University in the Sixties*, 372.

17. One example is perhaps illustrative. Charles Wheeler begins his account of the incident by saying that "one famous event was a sidewalk debate carried on between Murray Beja, of our Department, and Bernie Mehl, a professor in the School of Education with well-known libertarian views. He routinely gave all of his students A's, I was told, because anything else was elitist and demeaning to them" ("O. S. U.," page 4). Mehl, who was accompanied by a group of his students, confronted Beja as a toady of the administration for wearing the green ribbon. As Beja defended himself and the program, their "debate" attracted a large crowd of at least a few dozen spectators. There was and could not be a resolution to the discussion. After it, Beja, who had scheduled a graduate seminar to meet at his home that evening (the students were willing, even eager, to hold the seminar, but they did not want to cross picket lines), went home, where he found out that President Fawcett had closed the University. In his mail, too, was a two-sentence letter from a former student, who had failed his course the previous quar-

FIGURE 5.10. The Ohio National Guard on Campus, Spring 1970

science professor Louis Nemzer observed that after a series of meetings during the 12 days the university was shut down, 'there is more cohesion and more involvement by the faculty than I have seen in my 25 years at the university.'"[18]

Tensions were exacerbated on May 14 when two African American students were killed by police at Jackson State, Mississippi. OSU stayed shut until May 19, when it opened with thousands of Ohio National Guard troops surrounding the campus, rifles at the ready, and with a curfew imposed from midnight until 6:00 a.m. (The Guard began to withdraw May 29.)

---

ter, because he had stopped attending: "I am so lonely. Please help me." Beja broke down. He tried to phone the student's dorm, but all lines into OSU were tied up. He had time before the seminar was to start, so he got into his car and drove to the dorm, fearing the worst. When he arrived, the young man was packing to leave; his parents were to pick him up. They chatted for a while (and at subsequent get-togethers); it turned out that he had stopped attending class because of Eliot's "Prufrock" and "The Waste Land," both of which affected him greatly. He talked about how much he felt out of place and uncomfortable on the huge campus. (No doubt matters were exacerbated at Ohio State by its speedy and tremendous growth during the sixties: between 1960 and 1970 student enrollment doubled, from 20,487 to 41,015. Committee of Inquiry, "Spring Events," 5.)

Unfortunately, other members of the Department could of course cite their own stories of those troubled days.

18. Shkurti, *Ohio State University in the Sixties*, 328.

The Department, and then the University, decided that all students, graduate and undergraduate, could have the option if they chose of a grade of Satisfactory or Unsatisfactory, instead of the usual letter grades, for courses taken that quarter. Faculty Council also resolved that all undergraduate final exams be cancelled, and that regular classes be held during the week usually devoted to those exams. In June the Department determined that from then on all "graduate reports" (evaluations and descriptions of the work of graduate students in courses, that had always been strictly confidential) could now be open to students who wished to read their own reports. The representation on the Graduate Committee of graduate students was increased from one to three.

There were, certainly within the Department, attempts at more drastic experiments for change. Among its recommendations, the report of the Committee of Inquiry argued that an experimental program "should be designed and implemented in which the attempt is made to remove evaluation from teaching to the extent that it is a hindrance. Far too much of our teaching is toward, not learning, but grading."[19] As if in response to that recommendation, but before the report appeared, three members of the Department proposed to teach courses in which the students would grade themselves. That was only one part of the experiment, and was short-lived, but the faculty members felt that they accomplished something valuable. As Julian Markels writes in his memoir:

> In the summer of 1970, I had some long talks with two colleagues, my friend Gordon Grigsby and my new wife Joan Webber, about changing our entire manner of teaching. Then we three informed Al Kuhn that we would be conducting a new experiment in our autumn classes and would write reports on this experiment for our colleagues to see.
>
> On the first day of class that autumn, each of us distributed the customary course syllabus . . . and we explained to the students that they were free to take the course in this traditional format. But then we also explained that they were free to modify this format to suit their personal interests, aversions, and preferred ways of learning. In my American Renaissance course, for example, *The Scarlet Letter* and *Moby-Dick* were both listed readings. But if you felt suffocated for the moment by *The Scarlet Letter* from previous high school or college courses, you could skip it here and read *Moby-Dick* more lovingly. . . . And if at this moment in your life the prospect of writing still more three-page analytical papers looked as unproductive as reading *The Scarlet Letter* again, you could keep a journal, write a research paper, paint a picture, or compose a song. There would be no examinations, and the course

---

19. Committee of Inquiry, "Spring Events," 197.

FIGURE 5.11. Stanley J. Kahrl

grade would be determined in a teacher-student conference where the student had the last word.

What rocked the boat most for some colleagues was letting the students grade themselves. As these people put it, that compromised the integrity of the grading system and cheapened the value of the B.A. degree.[20]

Actually, another controversial element involved the freedom not to write any papers, and that led to meetings and even a Department "retreat" that discussed whether all courses should require a writing component, and for at least a time that was required. But, as Markels points out, "a number of colleagues joined us in trying to modify the original conception without sacrificing its purpose and spirit."[21]

Amidst all the turmoil, the professional life of the Department, including its teaching—and its hiring—inevitably continued.

In 1969 Stanley J. Kahrl became the first Director of the Center for Medieval and Renaissance Studies, bringing with him the *Old English Newsletter*,

---

20. Markels, *From Buchenwald*, 91–92.
21. Markels, *From Buchenwald*, 93.

of which he was the editor. He had co-edited *Merry Tales of the Mad Men of Gotham* (1965) and *Essential Articles for the Study of Old English Poetry* (1968). His *Traditions of Medieval English Drama* appeared in 1974. For a time he was Associate Dean of the College of Humanities. Stan died suddenly in 1989, in Tennessee, while participating in a Civil War reenactment of the Battle of Franklin. As Chris Zacher and Paul E. Szarmach of the University of Western Michigan noted in their memorial for Stan in *Old English Notes,* he "died in the outdoors that he loved, pursuing one of his many interests that reflected his enthusiasm for drama and living re-creations of the past."[22]

Another 1969 appointment in medieval literature was that of Walter Scheps. His *Chaucer's Anti-Fable: Reductio ad Absurdum in the Nun's Priest's Tale* appeared in 1970; he was promoted to Associate Professor the next year. He left OSU for the State University of New York at Stony Brook in 1976.

A major presence within the Folklore program, Patrick B. Mullen, came to the Department in 1970. He was promoted to Associate Professor a couple of years later, and to full Professor in 1981. He is the author of numerous articles and chapters in books, and of, for example, *I Heard the Old Fishermen Say: Folklore of the Texas Gulf Coast* (1978); *Lake Erie Fishermen: Work, Identity, and Tradition* (with Timothy C. Lloyd, 1990); *Listening to Old Voices: Folklore, Life Stories, and the Elderly* (1992); and *The Man Who Adores the Negro: Race and American Folklore* (2008).

---

22. Zacher and Szarmach, "In Memoriam," 15.

FOLKLORE

Patrick Mullen and Amy Shuman

Folklore has always existed at the edges of the English Department; nonetheless, most of the folklore faculty and students see folklore as central to the interdisciplinary goals of the Department. Folklore research encompasses every area of English and American literature, and folklorists have been engaged in many of the interdisciplinary endeavors of the Department, including cultural theory, performance studies, gender studies, and narrative, among others. The Ohio State University's English Department has played a significant role in the history of the discipline, and the discipline of folklore has, in turn, been significant for the Department. The first faculty member in English at Harvard University, Sir Francis Child, was originally appointed as a professor of rhetoric and oratory and later appointed as a professor of English, where he devoted his research to the English ballad. His student George Lyman Kittredge, both a ballad and a Shakespeare scholar, was also a folklorist. OSU's folklore program continued this tradition with the work of Francis Lee Utley, a student of Kittredge.

The history of Folklore Studies in the English Department at Ohio State University is all about the professors who taught here. Francis Lee Utley started the process. He received his Ph.D. in 1936 at Harvard, where Professor Kittredge influenced Fran's interest in folklore and medieval literature. Fran began his first teaching job in 1935 at Ohio State, and he became Professor of English and Folklore in 1973. He was President of the American Folklore Society (AFS) in 1951–52, and one of the original Fellows of AFS.

The wide range of his folklore scholarship is indicated by the titles of some of his most significant publications, "Folk Literature: An Operational Definition," "The Study of Folk Literature: Its Scope and Use," "The Bible of the Folk," "The Linguistic Component of Onomastics," and "The Migration of Folktales: Four Channels to the Americas." He was equally at home in folklore, literature, anthropology, and linguistics. The breadth of his scholarship was a foundation for the teaching of folklore and the creation of new courses within the English Department. Several of his graduate students went on to illustrious academic careers, including D. K. Wilgus at UCLA and Bruce Rosenberg at Brown University.

Fran was a great literary folklorist, but he didn't do fieldwork. Ethnographic field research was becoming more significant in the 1960s and 70s as folklore studies became more influenced by anthropology. Fran wanted to hire someone whose academic training included both folklore and literature, and the English Department appointed Patrick B. Mullen as an Assistant Professor in 1969. Pat's Ph.D. is in English from the University of Texas, but his dissertation was based on ethnographic fieldwork that produced his first book, *I Heard the Old Fishermen*

Say: Folklore of the Texas Gulf Coast, which was followed by *Lake Erie Fishermen: Work, Identity, Tradition* (with Timothy C. Lloyd); *Listening to Old Voices: Folklore, Life Stories, and the Elderly; Juneteenth Texas: Essays in African-American Folklore* (co-editor); and *The Man Who Adores the Negro: Race and American Folklore.* Pat taught folklore and American literature in the English Department for forty years. He helped establish the Center for Folklore Studies at OSU and was the first Director of the Center.

Daniel R. Barnes began teaching in the English Department in 1968. Dan was especially known for his articles on American legend, proverbs, and the relationship of folklore and American literature, including "Some Functional Horror Stories on the Kansas University Campus," "Folktale Morphology and the Structure of *Beowulf,*" "The Bosom Serpent: A Legend in American Literature and Folklore," and "Interpreting Urban Legends." He is the author of over a hundred scholarly papers in numerous European and American academic journals. He founded *Motif: International Review of Research in Folklore & Literature* in 1981 and served as Editor for nine years. He also served as one of the editors of *Proverbium,* an international journal of the study of the proverb. He was a Fellow of the American Folklore Society, The Folklore Society (University College, London), International Society for Folk-Narrative Research, Emily Dickinson Society, and Academy of American Poets. In 1989, he was elected a Folklore Fellow by the Finnish Academy of Sciences and Letters. At Ohio State he was known as a brilliant teacher able to engage students with complex intellectual ideas while also entertaining them with his sharp sense of humor. One of his favorite classes was on the joke.

Amy Shuman started teaching at Ohio State in 1981, having just finished her Ph.D. in Folklore and Folklife at the University of Pennsylvania, where she studied with Barbara Kirshenblatt-Gimblett, Dan Ben-Amos, John Szwed, and Erving Goffman. Her background in linguistic anthropology rather than literature and her ethnographic research on personal narrative in everyday life further developed the ethnographic focus of folklore at OSU. She turned her dissertation into her first book, *Storytelling Rights: Oral and Written Communication among Urban Adolescents.* Other books include *Other People's Stories: Entitlement Claims and the Critique of Empathy,* and *Rejecting Refugees: Political Asylum in the 21st Century.* With Charles Briggs she co-edited an influential special edition of *Western Folklore, Theorizing Folklore: Toward New Perspectives on the Politics of Culture.* Amy was the second director of the Center for Folklore Studies and was book review editor of the *Journal of American Folklore.* She also served as Director of Disability Studies and helped to develop a connection between folklore and disability studies. She received funding from the Wenner-Gren Foundation for Anthropological Research and a Guggenheim Fellowship to support her long-term research on the Italian marble carvers of Pietrasanta, Italy. Her publications in narrative, disability studies, political asylum, foodways, linguistic anthropology, and material culture all integrate folklore research. She is also a Fellow of the American Folklore Society.

Dorothy Noyes joined the English Department as a folklorist in 1996. She is a graduate of the University of Pennsylvania, where she studied with Roger Abrahams. Dorry conducted extensive ethnographic research on a Corpus Christi festival in Berga, a province of Catalonia, resulting in her book: *Fire in the Plaça: Catalan Festival Politics After Franco.* Dorry has published widely, on topics including heritage culture, the concept of the group (of central importance to folklorists), festival, and the fairytale. Her second book, *Humble Theory: Folklore's Grasp on Social Life*, was published in 2016. As director of the Center for Folklore Studies from 2005 until 2014, she led the development of a core graduate curriculum and created the Graduate Interdisciplinary Specialization in Folklore. She is a Fellow of the American Folklore Society.

Ray Cashman joined the English Department as a folklorist in 2006. He is a graduate of Indiana University, where he studied with Henry Glassie and Richard Bauman. His book, *Storytelling on the Northern Irish Border: Characters and Community,* represents his ethnographic study of the community of Aghyaran, a mixed Catholic-Protestant border community in Northern Ireland. His second book, *Packy Jim: Folklore and Worldview on the Irish Border,* continued his study of narrative, local character, and Irish folklore. He is also the co-editor of *The Individual and Tradition: Folkloristic Perspectives.* Ray served as Director of the Center for Folklore Studies before leaving to teach folklore at Indiana University in 2015, and during his tenure as Director, he created two graduate fellowships in folklore, a significant development in the establishment of folklore at OSU. He is editor of *The Journal of Folklore Research.*

Merrill Kaplan, who also came in 2006, holds a joint appointment in the Department of English and the Department of Germanic Languages and Literatures. She received her Ph.D. at the University of California, Berkeley, where she studied with Alan Dundes. She is a specialist in Old Norse-Icelandic literature and folklore and nineteenth-century Norwegian literature and culture. Merrill is a philologist, a textual specialist, as well as a scholar of internet folklore. Her book *Thou Fearful Guest: Addressing the Past in Four Tales in Flateyjarbók*, represents her extensive research on the Medieval Icelandic Saga.

From Fran Utley's day until Dan and Pat first joined the Department in the late sixties, there was only one folklore course, English 670, which could be taken for advanced undergraduate or graduate credit. The courses were expanded in the early seventies into separate undergraduate and graduate courses, including

English 270: Introduction to Folklore, which was taught in multiple sections as faculty in folklore expanded and graduate students in Folklore Studies began to teach introductory courses.

With the initiation of the Introduction to Folklore course, Pat Mullen created a folklore archive to store the collection projects undertaken by the students. The archive supplemented the record collection begun by Fran Utley that included more than 6,000 LPs from all over the world and a collection of over 20,000 books, now housed in the OSU library, from Fran's collection, one of the largest collections of folklore texts in the world. Begun in the 1970s, Ohio State's folklore archive is one of the oldest in the country. Over the years, several scholars donated materials to the archive, including Rosemary Joyce, who received her Ph.D. from the Department, and John Stewart, who taught in the Department as a creative writer. John Stewart arranged for the donation of material collected by Professor Priscilla Tyler of the University of Missouri. That collection includes over 4000 items of African and Caribbean folklore and literature. The Department of English provided funds for a 25% Graduate Associate to serve as the archivist. Recently, the archive received a $100,000 grant to digitize the materials. The archive is a treasure trove of knowledge about many topics, such as life in Ohio, youth culture, family customs, and several genres of oral performance, from jokes to narratives. Also, the collections include what are understood as "first usage" of slang, appearing in the archive collection before they appear in literature, film, television, or popular music.

When the Center for Folklore Studies was created, in July 1991, under the auspices of the Department of English, folklorists across campus were able to coordinate course offerings. The majority of folklore faculty remained in the Department of English, which had always admitted a few graduate students who identified folklore as a focus area. Initially, folklore at OSU had been divided between the Departments of English and Anthropology; two of the cultural anthropology faculty members were folklorists. When they retired, they were not replaced, leaving a gap in the teaching of ethnographic field methods, which was filled for many years by the folklorists in the Department of English. The English Department folklore faculty taught most of the qualitative ethnographic research courses on campus, and over the years, the folklore faculty served on dissertation committees for students in anthropology, communications, sociology, education, and other departments.

Being part of the Department of English, rather than existing as a free-standing unit, has had its advantages for folklorists at OSU. The faculty has enjoyed a great deal of autonomy in deciding what courses to offer, and as a result, the course offerings have represented a mix of standard core issues of folklore scholarship and innovative interdisciplinary ideas. OSU offers a Graduate

Interdisciplinary Specialization in folklore, and OSU students are widely regarded as among the best prepared in the world. We have had several visiting international scholars. The downside of being part of another unit is that our students, even in high-level courses, are often new to the field. However, the mix of expertise that students bring to us is, on the whole, conducive to better exchanges.

Until recently, we admitted very few students to do graduate work in folklore, and yet dozens of students have received Ph.D.'s in the field at OSU. Typically, students take a class without knowing much about the field but then decide to immerse themselves in it.

The creation of the Center for Folklore Studies did not change the fact that most of the faculty and most of the courses were still within the Department of English. However, it did provide greater international recognition of the program, which until then had rested entirely on the significant reputations of the individual faculty members. Folklore is an established discipline; the American Folklore Society was founded in 1888, and all of the folklore faculty and many of the students at OSU attend its annual meetings. The connection between folklore and English is long-standing. Although the Department of English remains central to folklore studies at OSU, the creation of the Center provided a means to develop an international and interdisciplinary program that eventually included faculty in East Asian, Near Eastern Languages and Literatures (especially Tunisian, Persian, Turkish, and Afghani), Slavic, Ethnomusicology, Nigerian, Irish, Italian, Catalonian, Nicaraguan, Trinidadian, Icelandic and Nordic, African and African American Studies, and Greek and Latin folklore and mythology.

Like any discipline, the field of folklore has seen major paradigm shifts over the past decades. When folklore was established at Ohio State, many scholars in the US identified themselves as either textual or ethnographic researchers. For a time, ethnographic research became dominant, but today students are equally interested in textual research, and several OSU scholars study the fairytale. Folklorists are constantly redefining themselves, finding new modes of interdisciplinary collaboration, and differentiating themselves from other researchers with similar interests in either cultural or textual studies. The OSU English Department has provided a supportive environment for folklore studies; the fields of English and American literature and folklore are not as concordant as they were in the days of Child, Kittredge, and Utley; folklorists no longer accept the designations of low and high culture that sustained the relationship between folklore and literature from the 1850s to the 1960s. Even (or especially) the concept of tradition, once a stalwart of folklore scholarship, is the subject of critique. In some ways folklorists today, as students of textual production and performance, find relevance in every area of English Department research.

FIGURE 5.12. James L. Battersby

FIGURE 5.13. Thomas Cooley

James L. Battersby, a scholar of eighteenth-century literature and of critical theory, as well as of higher education, also came to OSU in 1970, as an Associate Professor (he was promoted in 1982). He was a long-standing and dedicated participant in the group of literary theorists within the Department. Among his books are *Typical Folly: Evaluating Student Performance in Higher Education* (1973); *Rational Praise and Natural Lamentation: Johnson, Lycidas, and Principles of Criticism* (1980); *Paradigms Regained: Pluralism and the Practice of Criticism* 1991); and, after his retirement in 1995, *Reason and the Nature of Texts* (1996) and *Unorthodox Views: Reflections on Reality, Truth, and Meaning in Current Social, Cultural, and Critical Discourse* (2002).

Thomas Cooley also arrived in 1970, and was promoted to Associate Professor in 1976 and to Professor in 2000. He is the author of *Educated Lives: The Rise of Modern Autobiography in America* (1976) and *The Ivory Leg in the Ebony Cabinet: Madness, Race, and Gender in Victorian America* (2001). The latest version of his critical edition of *Adventures of Huckleberry Finn* will appear in 2019. Since his retirement in 2003, he has continued to work on the unpublished letters of Sophia Hawthorne and on new editions of various titles in rhetoric and composition, including *The Norton Sampler, The Norton Guide to Writing*, and *Back to the Lake*.

Throughout the years, the Department has been home to a number of distinguished visiting faculty. In 1970–71, and again in 1975–76, the Department hosted Fritz Senn, who is probably the most respected—and loved— "Joycean" in the world. At the time of his initial visiting appointment, Senn was contemplating pursuing an academic career, but he decided instead to remain in his home city of Zürich, where he started the Zürich James Joyce Foundation, which is still thriving. But his turn at teaching was markedly successful, and his graduate seminar on Joyce was very popular; he also on his own led an informal seminar on *Finnegans Wake,* which was so demanding that the Department decided to award graduate credit to all the students who participated in it. A couple of years after Senn's first visit, another important figure in Irish studies, Maurice Harmon, was a visiting professor while Morris Beja was a visiting faculty member at University College Dublin, Harmon's own institution.

Another Americanist, Suzanne Ferguson, came to the Department in 1971. *The Poetry of Randall Jarrell* appeared that year, and she was promoted to Associate Professor two years later. She left in 1983 to become Chair at Wayne State University, and became Dean of Humanities, Arts, and Social Sciences at Case Western Reserve in 1989. An especially talented musician on the viola de gamba, she co-authored a history of that instrument published in 2013.

Dudley Hascall, a linguist who was hired in 1972, had a difficult life and career. As Julian Markels records in his memoir (without naming Hascall), "a beloved colleague whose marriage broke up began coming to class drunk at 10 a.m. and soon committed suicide."[23]

After Al Kuhn had taken a sabbatical year for research in London, during which time John Gabel was the Acting Chair, President Fawcett asked Al to serve as Acting Vice President for Academic Affairs during Fawcett's last year in the presidency. The new president, Harold Enarson, asked him to stay in that position while he reorganized, and then to stay on as Provost; his official title was Provost and Vice President for Academic Affairs. Among his many accomplishments as Provost was setting up the Office of Women's Studies. He remained Provost until 1979; in 1985, he became Director of the University's Honors program until he retired in 1989. He died in 2012.

When he retired, the building housing the Honors program—which had in earlier years served as the residence of University presidents—was renamed The Albert J. Kuhn Honors and Scholars House.

---

23. Markels, *From Buchenwald*, 117.

CHAPTER 6

Mentor

The Gabel Years

CLEARLY, STEPPING INTO the job of Chair in the early 1970s called for a steady person of exceptional abilities and strength, inner and outer. John B. Gabel was universally recognized as the inevitable choice. Jim Phelan, in his *Beyond the Tenure Track,* as he mentions the course that was once Dick Altick's English 980, the required course in methods of bibliography, provides a capsule sense of how John was viewed by his colleagues, of his own generation and beyond:

> John Gabel is an elder statesman of the department, someone who got his Ph.D. here, who has been chair, who has been on virtually every important university committee, who has been acting dean of the graduate school. He is a meticulous man, always neat, always organized, always attentive to detail—in short someone ideally suited to teaching the course. He is also one of the most widely respected members of the department, the kind of person whose opinion and judgment carry weight with the rest of us.[1]

As we mentioned in the previous chapter, Gabel returned to OSU in 1965 after a time at the University of Illinois. He had received his OSU Ph.D. in 1961 (having attained an M.A. here in 1954, and then another from Wheaton Col-

---

1. Phelan, *Beyond the Tenure Track,* 34.

lege in 1957). He served as Acting Chair ("Chairman" in those days, of course) while Al Kuhn had a sabbatical in 1971–72, assuming that post in his own right in 1972 and retaining it until 1976.

One of John's earliest innovations was done quietly. It had long (always?) been a tradition at Promotion and Tenure evening meetings for the Chair to provide liquor during the Department's often lengthy deliberations. John realized that practice entailed legal as well as ethical problems, and he stopped it. The no doubt equally long tradition of heavy cigar smoking during the meetings took longer to disappear. In earlier years, too, the Committee on Promotion and Tenure had made recommendations to the entire senior professoriate without offering very much information about each candidate, but now the senior faculty were provided with more and more information—a complete c.v., copies of reviews of published work, evidence about teaching effectiveness and service—gradually adding up to the voluminous dossiers eventually required by both the College and the University.

Like all Chairs, John Gabel paid particular attention to faculty hires. Michelle Herman has mentioned as a "significant date in creative writing history" the hiring of Ernest Lockridge in 1971. He came here from Yale as an Associate Professor (tenured the following year and promoted in 1976). As a critic, he had already published *Twentieth Century Interpretations of The Great Gatsby: A Collection of Critical Essays* (1968). His first novel, *Prince Elmo's Fire*, came out in 1974, and his second, *Flying Elbows*, the next year. His works of non-fiction include *Travels with Ernest: Crossing the Literary/Sociological Divide* (with his wife, OSU Professor of Sociology Laurel Richardson, 2004) and *Skeleton Key to the Suicide of My Father Ross Lockridge, Jr., Author of Raintree County* (2011). After his retirement in 1991 he pursued his artistic career in painting as well as writing.

Another appointment in 1971 was that of Mark Auburn, a scholar of eighteenth-century literature, as an Assistant Professor; he was promoted in 1977, the year he published both *Sheridan's Comedies, Their Contexts and Achievements,* and, with his colleague Katherine H. Burkman, *Drama through Performance.* In 1981 he edited an edition of John Dryden's *Marriage à la Mode.* He served as Associate Vice Provost for the College of Arts and Sciences before leaving Ohio State in 1984 to become Vice President for planning at the University of Arkansas System, then Dean of the College of Arts and Sciences at Arkansas State University. He served as Vice Chancellor for Academic Affairs at Indiana University-Purdue University at Fort Wayne. At the University of Akron he became Senior Vice President and Provost and, later, Dean of the College of Fine and Applied Arts.

FIGURE 6.1. John B. Gabel

An emotional crisis occurred for the Department in 1973, when Assistant Professor John Williams, who had been hired in 1970, attempted suicide by taking an overdose of medication. Although a number of friends within the Department had offered him support, including Jim Battersby, Tom Cooley, and Murray Beja, John had not been able to finish his dissertation for Indiana University, and OSU had to inform him that his contract would not be renewed for another year. The suicide attempt left him in a near-comatose condition. His wife, Marilyn, decided that they should return to their home state of Massachusetts, where after a few years John died (and Marilyn then returned to Columbus to be with her supportive friends).

What turned out to be an especially complex appointment was that of Oscar Ronald Dathorne, in 1972, in African and African American literature. He had taught at the University of Sierra Leone and held various posts at Yale, Howard, and the University of Wisconsin before coming to Ohio State as a full Professor. Among his books were *The Black Mind: A History of African Literature* (1974) and *African Literature in the Twentieth Century* (1976). There was an awkward time when it was discovered that, while on paid leave from

OSU, he had accepted and assumed a position at the University of Miami. He officially left OSU in 1978.

Also hired in 1972 was someone who came to make a major mark within the Department, Marlene Longenecker, who was promoted to Associate in 1978. Marlene did not publish a great deal, but her accomplishments in both teaching—of eighteenth- and nineteenth-century literature, women's literature, and other fields—and service were stellar. She twice received the University Alumni Award for Distinguished Teaching and served in many capacities within the Department, including directing both Undergraduate and Graduate Studies. She served a term as Director of Women's Studies (see Valerie Lee on "Women's and Gender Studies" in chapter 8), and took a leave of absence of several years to work for the Governor of Ohio, Dick Celeste. Even after her retirement in 2008, she continued her service within the Department in various capacities, including scheduling courses, until 2013. After a long illness, she died in 2014, in her native California.

It was understandable that John Gabel—who would become Acting Dean of the Graduate School after his term as Chair—was especially interested in the development of the Department's graduate program. The entire program was streamlined during his term: in 1970 a total of 159 students were admitted as graduate students (120 as M.A. students, 29 as Ph.D. students); by 1977, the total was roughly halved (75 total, with 54 M.A. and 21 Ph.D. students).[2]

The character of the program changed in other important ways. For example, the formerly strict requirements in regard to philology and linguistics or the history of the language (five hours on the M.A. level, ten hours on the Ph.D. level) were removed in 1972. And the Ph.D. "General Examinations" were revised to lessen the overwhelming dominance of historical periods. One constant was that new members of the Department were assigned graduate courses relatively early in their careers and did not come up for tenure and promotion without having taught graduate students.

There were also important changes in the undergraduate program. A particularly innovative one was the way the advisers for English majors were chosen. The instructor for English 302, Critical Writing, required for all majors, became the student's adviser, thus assuring some degree of familiarity between the student and adviser. Each section of the course was limited to fifteen students. Only members of the professoriate taught the course, which students were urged—not always successfully, unfortunately—to take as early in their major programs as possible.

---

2. Suzanne Ferguson, memo on "Autumn Graduate Registration in English."

FIGURE 6.2. Marlene Longenecker

The entire undergraduate curriculum was revised during the 1976–77 academic year, curtailing some traditional period courses and introducing other courses that stressed themes and genres, and providing model programs for students aimed at, for example, graduate school, or law school. All these changes occurred during a period of decline in the number of English majors, for example from 396 in 1974 to 230 in 1978.[3]

Of course, the social life of the Department continued apace. An annual picnic occurred in the Spring. We have mentioned Al Kuhn playing charades: such games were common throughout the 1970s and into the 1980s, sometimes after one of the many dinner parties and sometimes at parties dedicated to those games. Occasionally there would be Halloween costume parties, or Christmas caroling parties such as those hosted by David and Joanne Frantz, or the New Year's parties hosted by Dan Barnes and Holly Downing until they moved to Coshocton.

Another continuing tradition was inviting prominent academics to be visiting faculty. The eminent British Dickensian Michael Slater, for example,

3. Beja et al., "Report of the Self-Study Committee," 28.

became "Distinguished Visiting Professor" twice, the first time in 1975. He was especially popular as a teacher and colleague. He learned to drive while in Columbus, in the process crashing Tom Cooley's car into a tree. Michael, who is gay, enjoyed telling how a driving instructor would joke with him, while they drove around campus, about how much he must enjoy being around all those coeds.

The expanding Creative Writing program hired William Allen in 1973. He was promoted to Associate Professor in 1979. His key role in instituting the M.F.A. has been discussed in Michelle Herman's account in Chapter 5 of this history. Allen published both fiction (for example, the novel *To Tojo from Billy-Bob Jones,* 1977) and non-fiction (such as *Starkweather: The Story of a Mass Murderer,* 1976, and *Walking Distance: An Ohio Odyssey,* 1990).

Another development of major importance for the future of Creative Writing on the Columbus campus was the appointment, in 1974, of David Citino as a faculty member on the Marion campus, where he would stay until he was hired for the Columbus campus in 1985. David received his Ph.D. from OSU in 1974 with a critical dissertation (*From Pemberley to Eccles Street: Families and Heroes in the Fiction of Jane Austen, Charles Dickens, and James Joyce*). He went on to concentrate on his poetry, eventually becoming the Poet Laureate of The Ohio State University; more on David Citino in chapter 8.

As part of Gabel's campaign to strengthen the program in rhetoric and composition, in 1975 he hired Susan Miller as an Associate Professor. Andrea Lunsford mentions in her account of rhetoric and composition in chapter 5 how Miller "swept into the job with enormous energy, intellect, and—almost immediately—controversy." Part of the controversy stemmed from the reluctance on the part of some faculty to see the field assume (or, really, resume) a major role within the Department—a controversy suggested by the subtitle of one of her books, *Textual Carnivals: The Politics of Composition* (1991). Other works of hers influential in the teaching of writing included *Rescuing the Subject: A Critical Introduction to Rhetoric and the Writer* (1989) and *The Norton Book of Composition Studies* (2009). Her impact within the Department was real, although she left OSU after only three years—first for the University of Wisconsin-Milwaukee and then the University of Utah, where she was the founding director of the University Writing Program. She died of cancer in 2013.

John Gabel left the post of Chair in 1976. He served as the Acting Dean of the Graduate School 1984–85. His contribution to the *History of the Ohio State University,* the volume *The Jennings Years, 1981–1990,* appeared the year of his retirement, 1992. In his last years John valiantly fought Parkinson's Disease. He died in 2012, survived by his wife of fifty-seven years, Betty.

CHAPTER 7

The Socialist Professor as Chair

The Markels Years

TWO PEOPLE who have served as Chair of the English Department have published memoirs that cover at least part of their careers: Julian Markels and James Phelan. The authors of this book strongly recommend both volumes for what they reveal about life within the Department during the years their memoirs cover. Only Julian's book—*From Buchenwald to Havana: The Life and Opinions of a Socialist Professor*—speaks about his years as Chair, in a chapter titled "Adventures in Middle-Management: Columbus, 1976–83" and which begins, "When I became chair of the Ohio State University English Department on July 1, 1976, a week after my 51st birthday, I'd been a member of the department for twenty years."[1]

Early in his tenure as Chair, the Department undertook a "self-study," as far as we can determine the first in its history, or, anyway, the first to be called that. The process, which began in 1976 and produced a report in 1978, was headed by a committee of six members: five faculty (Morris Beja, its chair, David Frantz, James Kincaid, Melanie Lusk, and Julian Markels), and Mary Jo Hlay, a graduate student.[2] Also participating in various of its activities were

---

1. Markels, *From Buchenwald*, 111.

2. A side note: Mary Jo, as Mary Jo Markey, went to Hollywood and became a prominent film editor. She was nominated for an Academy Award in 2016 for *Star Wars: The Force Awakens*; we've been told that had she won, she intended in her acceptance speech to thank the OSU English Department.

FIGURE 7.1. Julian Markels

two undergraduates, William O'Neill and James Vradelis. A major role was also played by three outside examiners: Richard Lloyd Jones (University of Iowa), J. Hillis Miller (Yale University), and Robert Ornstein (Case Western Reserve University).

In this chapter and elsewhere we have cause to quote or refer to the 67-page report of the Self-Study Committee, which was the result of deliberations and consultations with the entire Department—faculty, students, staff, and alumni. The report by the outside examiners was to have been made after they left Columbus following their campus visit, but the Blizzard of '78, January 25–27, kept them in town and their hotel, so they took advantage of being trapped together to write their report before they left. As Markels recalls in his memoir, Columbus had

> twenty-seven inches of snow in three days. The classes we had arranged for them to attend were cancelled [Ohio State closed because of weather for the first time in its history], but not the dinner parties at faculty homes, and what I remember most about the self-study is spending our evenings that weekend pushing cars out of snow banks.[3]

3. Markels, *From Buchenwald*, 122.

The reports by the examiners and the committee led to a "Memorandum of Agreement" with the College of Humanities concerning a number of the recommendations in regard to funding, curriculum, and staffing we have already mentioned or will deal with later in this chapter. (A side effect for the two undergraduates was that, helped by their contacts with Hillis Miller, Bill and Jim were both admitted for graduate work at Yale.)

An important observation made by the Self-Study report was one about trends within the entire discipline:

> Literary study is being connected more functionally and more visibly with other studies, including the study of writing and composition pedagogy; and that is a lucky development both for students and faculty in a state university with the largest freshman English program in the country, and a faculty involved again in teaching composition.[4]

The largest such program in the country: and English 110, as it was then termed, was the only course required by every college in the University. Inevitably, therefore, a great deal of attention had to be paid—as it always had been—to the role within the Department of rhetoric and composition. That fact did not sit well with everyone in the Department. As Markels reports in his memoir:

> When I came up for re-election . . . the dean at that time conferred with my colleagues before reappointing me, and he told me that their one big criticism of my first-term performance was that I spent too much time on our writing program. Or as the old joke goes, an English department chair dies, goes to heaven, and is greeted by St. Peter at the Pearly Gates. "You've lived an honorable life," says Peter, "and you are eligible to enter. But I should also mention that if you should choose to enter rather than be hurled down below, you will still be held responsible for the writing program."
>
> Yet I also sensed that this program could be an opportunity as well as a burden. . . . My ambition was to make a difference in the daily life where our professional work was grounded, and the study and teaching of writing had always been a big part of this life.[5]

What had once been called "remedial composition" now gained increasingly professional attention and eventually received new terminology as well, such as "basic writing." In 1976, at a time when the University was begin-

---

4. Beja et al., "Report of the Self-Study Committee," 5.
5. Markels, *From Buchenwald*, 113.

ning to shift from fully open admissions to selective admissions, the Department instituted an experimental course, the Writing Workshop, with a pilot test group of ninety students. The results of the course, when compared to a control group of students with similar prior qualifications, were notably encouraging.

In line with those efforts was the appointment in 1977 of Sara Garnes, who had an OSU Ph.D. degree in Linguistics, to direct the Writing Workshop. Her dissertation was published as a book, *Quantity in Icelandic: Production and Perception*, in 1976. She was promoted to Associate Professor in 1973. Coming out of her work in Basic Writing was the co-edited volume *Writing Lives: Exploring Literacy and Community* (1996). She worked with Andrea Lunsford, then a Ph.D. student in the Department doing research in the realm of Basic Writing; both Julian and the Dean of the College of Humanities at the time, Arthur Adams, were very supportive of the program.

As Sara reports, "It was an exciting time in composition studies, so a lot of people wanted to get experience in teaching basic writing," and there was "a real sense of community." But, as we have said, some members of the Department were disturbed by the new developments: as Sara puts it, the feeling was that "there was the Rhet-Comp program, and then there was the 'real' English Department." Further complicating matters was tension between Sara and Frank O'Hare, who came to OSU in 1978 to direct First Year Writing; but after a time, "bless Julian, he said I could report directly to him."[6]

Policy decisions within the College of Humanities led to the eventual transformation of the Division of Comparative Literature into the Division (later the Department) of Comparative Studies and the consequent transfer of some faculty to other departments. As a result, in 1977 the Department of English gained Katherine H. Burkman as a tenured Associate Professor (she became a full Professor in 1985). She had already published *The Dramatic World of Harold Pinter: Its Basis in Ritual,* in 1971, a version of her 1968 OSU Ph.D. dissertation for the Department of Theater. We have already mentioned the volume she edited with Mark Auburn in 1977, *Drama through Performance.* She continued her interest in the study of performance in *Literature through Performance: Shakespeare's Mirror and a Canterbury Caper* (1978). *The Arrival of Godot: Ritual Patterns in Modern Drama* appeared in 1986. Among her other edited volumes are *Myth and Ritual in the Plays of Samuel Beckett* (1987) and *Pinter at Sixty* (1993). After her retirement in 1995 she continued her activities as a director of plays and a playwright (*I Don't Think So: Life's Stages, A Play Made up of 14 Monologues* appeared in 2010), as well as a critic

---

6. Sara Garnes, video interview with Andrew Smart, 2016.

and scholar (as with *The Drama of the Double: Permeable Boundaries*, 2016). She was also one of the founding members of the theatrical troupe, Women at Play.

Of course, other traditional areas were not overlooked in hiring decisions. Leslie Tannenbaum, a scholar of Romantic literature, was hired in 1977 and promoted in 1983, the year after his *Biblical Tradition in Blake's Early Prophecies: The Great Code of Art* appeared. In subsequent years, he also became active in the study and teaching of gay literature.

In fact, the Department now realized that it—like the profession—was heading in a number of new areas. As the Self-Study report recognized, the Department "has been for the most part traditionally historical," while

> developments have encouraged many within the profession to listen freshly to those of its members who were saying all along that historical studies constitute only one branch of the discipline—although a central one—and that we still need to discover a more comprehensive paradigm for the discipline as a whole.[7]

As a major part of that recognition, the Department made two important appointments in literary theory, also in 1977. James Phelan came with a Ph.D. from the University of Chicago. He was promoted to Associate Professor in 1978 and to full Professor in 1989; he became the Chair in 1994 (see chapter 9 of this history). He was the first person in the Department to receive both the Alumni Distinguished Teaching Award (2007) and the Distinguished Scholar Award (2004). *Worlds from Words: A Theory of Language in Fiction* (1981) and *Reading People, Reading Plots: Character, Progression, and the Interpretation of Narrative* (1989) were both published by the University of Chicago Press. Among his other books—in addition to a large number of edited volumes— are *Narrative as Rhetoric: Technique, Audiences, Ethics, Ideology* (1996); *Living to Tell about It: A Rhetoric and Ethics of Character Narration* (2005); and *Experiencing Fiction: Judgments, Progressions, and the Rhetorical Theory of Narrative* (2007). He edits *Narrative*, the journal of the International Society for the Study of Narrative, and, with Peter J. Rabinowitz and Robyn Warhol, co-edits the Ohio State University Press book series, The Theory and Interpretation of Narrative.

At this point, we provide Phelan's own account of the impact of critical theory on the Department.

---

7. Beja et al., "Report of the Self-Study Committee," 63, 2.

FIGURE 7.2. James Phelan

CRITICAL THEORY

James Phelan

The role of critical theory in the English Department reflects its role in the larger profession of English Studies over the last forty years. After the breakdown of the New Critical orthodoxy in the 1960s, the profession underwent a "theory revolution" in which a wide range of foundations for literary study—some of which denied the possibility of a foundation—were proposed and contested. Although no new dominant orthodoxy equivalent to the New Criticism emerged, the profession as a whole became theory-conscious, and every forward-thinking department made more room in its curriculum and often in its hiring for theory. By the 1990s, theory had become part and parcel of just about every subfield, and hiring in critical theory was no longer common.

The OSU English Department made its first faculty appointments in critical theory in 1977, under chair Julian Markels: Walter "Mac" Davis, hired at the Associate level, and me, hired as an Assistant Professor with a newly-minted Ph.D. Although 1977 also saw the departures of Jim Kincaid to the University of Colorado and Tom Mitchell to the University of Chicago, Mac and I entered a department in which theory was already prominent. Marlene Longenecker was actively engaged in the still-emerging conversations and controversies of feminist theory, and Jim Battersby was teaching a two-quarter seminar devoted to recent developments in theory. Jim also was coordinator of a well-attended and lively critical theory reading group.

Given this environment, Mac and I felt warmly welcomed, and soon the Department began to add theory offerings to the curriculum: "Studies in Critical

Theory" at both the graduate and undergraduate level, as well as a 900-level course to serve as a counterpart to English 980, the course in Bibliography and Method that had long been taught by Richard Altick. Mac's energy and charisma attracted many graduate students to the field. In addition, the Department decided to add instruction in critical theory to its "Introduction to Graduate Study" course. At first the Department split the introductory course and its five quarter-credits over two quarters. Autumn's two credits were devoted to learning about the range of work being done in the Department, through visits by faculty from the area groups, and to learning the library and its relevant resources. Winter's three credits were then devoted to learning about multiple aspects of critical theory, from how to analyze theoretical arguments to how to compare and contrast different approaches to the same text. In other words, Part Two tried to combine coverage (theory as a noun) and skill development (theory as a verb). Over time graduate students expressed reservations about the division: they found Autumn too light and Winter too heavy. As a result, the graduate faculty decided to make "Introduction to Graduate Study" a single five-credit course that gave students the basics of bibliography and focused primarily on theory. In addition, the Department agreed to fund an advanced Ph.D. student on a 25% appointment to be an additional resource for the first-year students. This format worked well from the late 1980s into the first decade of the twenty-first century, when the Department again adjusted the Introductory course to deemphasize coverage of theory as it focused on a broader range of activities relevant to advanced English Studies. Along with that shift, the Department has required that Ph.D. students take a course in theory beyond Introduction to Graduate Study.

In the 1980s, English was not the only department in the College of Humanities interested in expanding its theory offerings—Philosophy and all the other language and literature departments were as well—and, not surprisingly, turf battles arose. Were Derrida, Foucault, and Lacan the property of the French Department? Did German own Gadamer, Adorno, and Habermas? Or did they all belong to Philosophy? Was English poaching when it taught these thinkers? The answers depended on whom you asked—and where s/he was standing in the College. In order to address these issues, the Dean of the College, G. Micheal Riley, charged an ad hoc committee of faculty in the relevant departments to come up with a solution, and he appointed me as chair. The discussions were lively but most amicable, and we recommended that (a) individual departments have the autonomy to teach the theory they thought relevant for their students, and (b) interested departments should cross-list two courses, one on Foundations of Critical Theory (which would pair older theoretical texts with contemporary ones, e.g., Saussure's *Course in General Linguistics* and Derrida's *Of Grammatology*) and one on Contemporary Theory (which would take up current debates). These two courses served both the Department and the College well up until recently, when for various reasons, including a smaller Ph.D. program and the switch to semesters, we reduced the number of courses.

The important place of theory in the College was also underlined by Dean Riley's mandate to have a College-sponsored theory conference. During the 1980s, the College had set aside considerable funding for annual conferences. In 1981, for example, Murray Beja, Stan Gontarski (OSU-Lima), and Pierre Astier (Romance Languages) co-organized a very successful symposium on Samuel Beckett, and in 1984 Charles Klopp (Romance Languages) organized a conference on George Orwell's *1984*. Dean Riley and Chair Murray Beja then tapped me to organize a theory conference for 1986. That well-funded conference, "Narrative Poetics: Innovations, Limits, and Challenges," featured plenary addresses by Terry Eagleton, Wayne Booth, J. Hillis Miller, Seymour Chatman, Shoshana Felman, and Teresa de Lauretis. It also featured many participants brought in by what was then called the Society for the Study of Narrative Literature, and the overall success of the event prompted SSNL to host annual conferences. SSNL has evolved to become the International Society for the Study of Narrative, and its 2016 conference was in Amsterdam and its 2017—its thirty-second—in Lexington, Kentucky.

In the late 1980s, the Department made two other hires in critical theory, but one faculty member left and another did not earn tenure. By the mid-1980s, however, many new faculty hired in historical periods also had an expertise in critical theory, a trend that has continued to this day. Especially notable in this regard are Mark Conroy, Jon Erickson, Ethan Knapp, Sandra Macpherson, Roxann Wheeler, Brian McHale, Tommy Davis, and Jian Chen. This development, which reflects the integration of critical theory into literary and cultural studies more generally, meant that after the late 1980s the Department no longer searched for specialists in critical theory broadly conceived. Instead, when it has done a theory hire since then, the Department has searched for specialists in specific branches of theory, most notably, postcolonial theory, queer theory, disability studies, and narrative theory (see the account on Project Narrative in chapter 9; that account is very much a part of the history of critical theory in the Department, even as "narrative and narrative theory" has become its own distinct subfield).

Thus, over the last forty years, critical theory in the Department has gone from "the new Big Thing" to "Well-Established and Still Emerging Many Things." The larger lesson of this history is that, as theory's role in the profession continues to evolve, so too will its role in the Department.

As Jim mentions, another appointment in the field of theory in the same year, 1977, was Walter A. Davis ("Mac"), who came to OSU from the University of California, Santa Barbara, as an Associate Professor. Davis is the author of works in philosophy as well as cultural and literary criticism and theory. His first book, *The Act of Interpretation: A Critique of Literary Reason* (1978), was followed by *Inwardness and Existence: Subjectivity in/and Hegel, Heidegger, Marx, and Freud* (1989); *Get the Guests: Psychoanalysis, Modern American Drama, and the Audience* (1994); *Deracination: Historicity, Hiroshima, and the Tragic Imperative* (2001); and, after his retirement in 2002, *Death's Dream Kingdom: The American Psyche Since 9-11* (2006). He is also a dramatist (as well as an actor); his plays include *The Holocaust Memorial: A Play about Hiroshima* and *An Evening with JonBenet Ramsey*.

Jim Phelan testifies, with justice, that "Mac's energy and charisma attracted many graduate students" to study critical theory, and in many ways he was indeed consistently a presence in the English Department, always outspoken and frequently controversial. The College of Humanities had a series of "Inaugural Lectures" delivered by faculty members promoted to, or hired as, full Professors; the first was delivered, with notable success, by Pat Mullen, in 1981. For his promotion in 1988, which he regarded as overdue, Mac spoke with a paper bag over his head during the entire lecture, delivered in the grand lounge of the Faculty Club. In it he spoke scornfully about his colleagues—referring to himself as a Mozart surrounded by Salieris. He retired in 2002.

Frank O'Hare was appointed as a full Professor in 1978, to direct the program in Rhetoric and Composition. He was renowned as an expert in "sentence combining," and the National Council of Teachers of English had published his *Sentence Combining: Improving Student Writing without Formal Grammar Instruction* in 1973; he had also published *Sentencecraft: An Elective Course in Writing* in 1975. His *Modern Writer's Handbook* (1989) came out in a number of editions. His leadership of the program in Rhetoric and Composition was occasionally controversial, as the comment by Sara Garnes would suggest; occasionally too there would be tension between Julian and him. As David Frantz tells us, "One of my jobs as vice chair came to be sitting in on every meeting Julian had with Frank O'Hare to keep things from escalating."

One of Julian's innovations for relieving tensions was the off-campus "retreat." He describes its origin in his memoir:

Someone suggested that we launch our self-study with a weekend retreat at a state park before the new school year began. There was no budget for this, nor was there any precedent at that time for an off campus retreat. But to my surprise, people agreed to pay their own way, and we devoted each half-day's session at the retreat to a single aspect of the department's work: teaching; scholarship; undergraduate, graduate, and writing programs; departmental organization and government. The idea was to agree for each area on a general critique and guidelines for reform . . . and then to develop detailed proposals within these guidelines after we got home.[8]

The social aspects of the weekend were essential to getting work done: "Old timers and newcomers, scotch-drinkers and pot smokers, medievalists and Americanists, grilled food together and shared cabins in the woods and canoes on the lake. Some uptight liberals were persuaded to smoke a joint, and some shaggy insurgents were persuaded by the arguments of rock-ribbed conservatives."[9] (Some, not all.)

Another appointment made in 1978 was that of the medievalist Lisa J. Kiser, who was promoted to Associate Professor in 1983, and to full Professor in 1991. She distinguished herself as a teacher and colleague as well as a scholar, receiving the Alumni Award for Distinguished Teaching in 1990 and the Arts and Humanities Exemplary Faculty Award in 2002. In addition to essays and reviews, she is the author of two books on Chaucer, *Telling Classical Tales: Chaucer and the Legend of Good Women* (1983) and *Truth and Textuality in Chaucer's Poetry* (1991), and the editor, with Barbara A. Hanawalt of the Department of History, of *Engaging with Nature: Essays on the Natural World in Medieval and Early Modern Europe* (2008). Lisa is married to her colleague Jim Battersby. She retired in 2014.

We've mentioned that Katherine Burkman came to the Department from the Division of Comparative Studies. Julian tried, unsuccessfully, to get the Department to agree to bringing the entire division into the English Department. But the Department did gain Barbara Hill Rigney, in 1979, as an Associate Professor. She had received the Alumni Award for Distinguished Teaching before attaining her Ph.D., which was awarded by the Department in 1977; also distinctive was that when she walked into the oral defense of her dissertation, she was in the highly unusual position of already having a contract for its publication by the University of Wisconsin Press, which published *Madness and Sexual Politics in the Feminist Novel: Studies in Brontë, Woolf, Lessing, and Atwood* in 1978 and *Lilith's Daughters: Women and Religion in Contemporary Fiction* in 1982. She came out with two of the earliest book-length studies of a couple of major novelists: *Margaret Atwood* (1987) and *The Voices of Toni Morrison* (1991). On Barbara's role in the development of Women's Studies at OSU, see the account in chapter 8 by Valerie Lee.

---

8. Markels, *From Buchenwald*, 119.
9. Markels, *From Buchenwald*, 120.

FIGURE 7.3. Lisa J. Kiser

FIGURE 7.4. Barbara Hill Rigney

FIGURE 7.5. Amy Shuman

In 1981 the Department hired a faculty member in Folklore studies who went on to serve multiple important roles throughout the University and in the profession, Amy Shuman (who was promoted to Associate Professor in 1987, and to Professor in 2004). The account by Shuman and Pat Mullen of the role of Folklore within the Department appears in chapter 5 of this history. Her book-length studies include *Storytelling Rights: The Uses of Oral and Written Texts by Urban Adolescents* (1986); *Other People's Stories: Entitlement Claims and the Critique of Empathy* (2005); and, with Carol Bohmer, *Rejecting Refugees: Political Asylum in the 21st Century* (2008). She served simultaneously as the Director of the Center for Folklore Studies and as the Director of Disabilities Studies from 1995 until 2005. As we write, she is the Director of the Diversity and Identity Studies Collective and the Coordinator of the Human Rights Working Group sponsored by the Humanities Institute. She is also an affiliated faculty member of the Departments of Anthropology, Comparative Studies, and Women's, Gender, and Sexuality Studies.

Amy was awarded a Guggenheim Fellowship in 1989 and is a Fellow of the American Folklore Society. She has also received important awards within Ohio State University: the Arts and Humanities Exemplary Faculty Award in 2007, the Distinguished Scholar Award in 2015, and the Alumni Award for

Distinguished Teaching in 2016. She once performed another, little-known, service for her colleagues as well:

> Do you remember that there used to be bells that went off at the end and beginning of class in Denney Hall? When my first son was born (no maternity leave in those days), the first summer that I taught, I brought him to school with me with a babysitter to take care of him when I was in class. The bells were waking him up, so I arranged to have them turned off. They've been turned off ever since, since the summer of 1983.[10]

In 1979, Stanley Gontarski (an OSU Ph.D., then teaching at the Lima campus) and Morris Beja were attending an International James Joyce Symposium in Zürich, and over drinks at the James Joyce Pub, they threw out the idea that they ought to do a similar symposium on Samuel Beckett. Back at OSU, they took the idea seriously, and co-opted Pierre Astier of the Department of Romance Languages. The three of them approached Diether H. Haenicke, Dean of the College of Humanities, and he decided that the symposium would be the First Annual Symposium in the Humanities, held May 7–9, 1981, marking Beckett's seventy-fifth year. The first major international conference on Beckett, it attracted a large number of critics and scholars, including Deirdre Bair, Ruby Cohn, Hugh Kenner, and James Knowlson, and the publisher John Calder. It was tied with exhibits of Beckett manuscripts, editions, and photographs in the OSU Libraries, with a production of *Waiting for Godot* by the Department of Theater, and followed by a conference sponsored by the Theatre Research Institute, May 9–10, "Beyond Beckett: Post-Modern Theatre and Drama." The symposium itself presented professional productions of *Footfalls*, with Rosemary Pountney, and *A Piece of Monologue*, with David Warrilow.

But its coup was unprecedented: Beckett wrote an original play for the conference, and he even called it *Ohio Impromptu*. It was directed by Alan Schneider (who had directed the first American production of *Waiting for Godot*), with David Warrilow as Reader and Rand Mitchell as Listener.

The Graduate Associate for the symposium was Esther Rauch, a Ph.D. student in English. When a collection of essays coming out of the conference was published, it was dedicated to her.[11]

Over the years, of course, the Ph.D. program had undergone many changes. At this time, for the so-called General Examination (more or less

---

10. Amy Shuman, email to the authors, August 1, 2016.

11. Morris Beja, S. E. Gontarski, and Pierre Astier, eds. *Samuel Beckett: Humanistic Perspectives.* Columbus: Ohio State University Press, 1983.

the equivalent of what was later to be called the Candidacy Examination), the Department listed fifteen areas:

1. Old and Middle English Literature
2. English Renaissance Literature
3. Restoration and Eighteenth-Century Literature
4. Romantic and Victorian Literature
5. American Literature through the Nineteenth Century
6. Twentieth-Century American and British Literature
7. Poetry
8. Prose Fiction
9. Drama
10. Criticism
11. Linguistics
12. Rhetoric
13. Folklore
14. Technical Bibliography and Textual Criticism
15. Another field within or without the Department, to be designated by the student's major adviser: for example, another literature (may be limited by period, such as Nineteenth-Century French), Women's Studies, history (may be limited by period), tragedy, cinema, fine arts (including architecture), and the like.

Five of the first six areas had to be represented either in the student's course work or the General Examination, which consisted of four parts; at least two of the parts had to be in examinations in the first nine areas.

As always, there were budget restrictions and problems. The Department could not afford to buy a photocopier, although, as Markels reports in his memoir, "A faculty wife surgeon gave the department its first Xerox machine in honor of her husband's birthday, and this socialist restricted its use to faculty but not graduate students or we couldn't afford the paper."[12] For many faculty, a major setback had occurred when the English Department Library ceased being able to buy books; it now lost its modest serial budget as well. As a result, it became a reading room rather than a full library.

At the time of the Self-Study, the Department consisted of "70 regular faculty, 27 part-time or temporary faculty, and 115 Graduate Teaching

---

12. Markels, *From Buchenwald*, 116.

Associates."[13] GTAs normally taught one composition class each quarter as a "fifty-percent appointment," ostensibly meaning twenty hours per week in class preparation, teaching, office hours, and grading themes—a workload the Self-Study pointed out was "euphemistic."[14]

The difficulties faced by the "part-time or temporary faculty" were even more pronounced in some ways, and their role was becoming increasingly important, even essential, to the workings of the Department. "Adjunct faculty"—another euphemism—were becoming progressively more numerous throughout the academic world, and the OSU English Department was no exception. The Department's own Frank Donoghue would later argue in *The Last Professors: The Corporate University and the Fate of the Humanities* that professors were becoming an endangered species, with the university "evolving in ways that make their continued presence unnecessary, even undesirable," with tenure itself becoming a "receding feature in the landscape of academic labor."[15] The OSU Department did not lose tenure, nor did it stop hiring tenure faculty: far from it. But it was becoming more and more dependent on adjunct faculty.

The Department continued to hire—but it had its scares. Julian was able to offer a position in American Literature to Steven S. Fink in 1983, by phone. But before he was able to get a written document to Steve, the University imposed a hiring freeze and at first would not recognize Julian's oral offer as binding, even though Steve had let his other prospects know that he had accepted a position. There was a tense period before Julian was able to get the University to agree to consider the offer a legitimate one. Steve went on to be promoted to Associate Professor in 1989, teaching American Literature, American Studies, and Jewish American Literature; to serve as Vice Chair of the Department; and to be Associate Executive Dean of Arts and Sciences. His *Prophet in the Marketplace: Thoreau's Development as a Professional Writer* was published by Princeton in 1992 and reissued by the OSU Press in 1999, the same year he co-edited, with Susan Williams, *Reciprocal Influences: Literary Production, Distribution, and Consumption in America.*

Julian gave up the Chair in 1983, and retired in 1991. He continued to publish scholarship, as well as his 2012 memoir. *Melville and the Politics of Identity: From King Lear to Moby-Dick* came out in 1993, and *Negotiating an Audience for American Exceptionalism: Redburn and Roughing It* in 1999.

---

13. Beja et al., "Report of the Self-Study Committee," 7.
14. Beja et al., "Report of the Self-Study Committee," 48.
15. Donoghue, *Last Professors*, xi, 55.

FIGURE 7.6. Steven S. Fink

He led a department that, as the final paragraph of the Self-Study asserted, was "notably free of distrust, political infighting, and bitter cliques. To be sure, and to put it mildly, we continue to have our disagreements and disputes and disappointments; but through them all there is a general consensus that we can face them with a spirit of cooperation and confidence in our mutual good will that, unfortunately, sometimes seems all too unusual in our profession."[16]

16. Beja et al., "Report of the Self-Study Committee," 67.

CHAPTER 8

The Omnibus English Department

The Beja Years

A NUMBER of administrators in the College of Humanities and the central administration believed that the Department should pursue excellence and an enhanced reputation by concentrating its resources in one or maybe two fields. Within the English Department itself a few faculty argued that some of the most prestigious departments had followed that path in order to achieve their eminent status, even at the cost of lessening the role of, and perhaps even eliminating, whole programs, not excluding traditional ones. In contrast, like most of the faculty in the Department, Morris Beja, who became Chair in 1983, held the conviction—rightly or wrongly—that a department as large as OSU's, at the flagship university of the state, could achieve prominence and indeed greatness only by recognizing the responsibilities of its size and role within the state and nation, by including within its faculty and program every major field and many or most burgeoning fields within the expanding discipline that was now "English." Joined to that sense was a determination to increase diversity within the Department. The term that came to encapsulate that view referred to OSU's as an "omnibus" department.

As the Self-Study early in Julian Markels's tenure as Chair reflected, an "English" Department traditionally meant the study of literature, language, rhetoric, and perhaps creative writing and folklore. In the eighties, the Department hired in those fields—but also in Feminist Studies, African American Studies, Chicano-Chicana Studies, Gay and Lesbian Studies, Postcolonial

FIGURE 8.1. Morris Beja

Studies, Cultural Studies, and Film, while also making appointments in the Renaissance, the Romantics, early American literature, and Modernism, for example.

The Department was able to hire a good many faculty in those years, although at first with imposed restrictions. A notable problem was a continuing though relatively new College policy that all appointments were to be limited to three years, renewable, a policy that created problems of morale within the Department and special problems in recruiting new faculty. The restrictions were soon lifted, but policies leading to the proliferation of adjunct faculty persisted, even as the Department participated in record numbers of tenure-track appointments. Many efforts to provide adjunct faculty with some measure of security and benefits often ran against policies not only at the College and University level, but also in the University Senate. Efforts to provide reliable employment and benefits for non-regular faculty did not attain a measure of success until the twenty-first century.

During the first year of Beja's tenure as Chair (that was the term now, not Chairman), a newsletter began to be distributed outside the Department and

FIGURE 8.2. *Impromptu,* vol. 4, no. 1, Autumn 1986

University as well as within them. The first issue of *Impromptu* (the name obviously a nod to Samuel Beckett) appeared in the Autumn of 1983, edited by Arnold Shapiro, who continued in that role until his retirement in 1992, when he was succeeded by Leslie Tannenbaum (and later by Brenda Brueggemann and Lisa Tatonetti); over 5,000 print copies of each issue were distributed to alumni, faculty, students, and friends of the English Department.

David Frantz agreed to continue as Vice Chair. He and Arnie Shapiro served as Director of Undergraduate Studies in that capacity, and they both were key to the process of hiring new faculty, in both searching for and recruiting the best prospects for the Department.

In the area of Linguistics, Terence Odlin was appointed in 1984 and promoted to Associate Professor in 1990. He is the author of *Language Transfer: Cross-Linguistic Influence in Language Learning* (1989; published in Japanese in

1995); and editor or co-editor of *Perspectives on Pedagogical Grammar* (1994), *Language Contact, Variation and Change* (1998), and *Studies of Fossilization in Second Language Acquisition* (2006). Terry retired in 2011.

Phoebe Spinrad was also appointed in 1984 and promoted in 1990. She came to academe with what was at the time the unusual background of having been a Captain in the military. A scholar of the Renaissance, she is the author of *The Summons of Death on the Medieval and Renaissance English Stage* (1987) and of articles on medieval and Renaissance drama and poetry, and on the literature and history of the war in Vietnam. Phoebe retired in 2009.

The 1978 Self-Study lamented the regularity with which a number of faculty within the Department had been wooed by other universities. That pattern then began to shift, and OSU was doing the raiding. For example, John Stewart came to the Department in 1985 as a full Professor and as a triple threat in Folklore, African American literature, and creative writing. That same year, David Riede was recruited from the University of Rochester, bringing strengths in Romantic and Victorian poetry and poetics. Among his books are *Dante Gabriel Rossetti and the Limits of Victorian Vision* (1983; and *Dante Gabriel Rossetti Revisited*, 1992), *Matthew Arnold and the Betrayal of Language* (1988), *Oracles and Hierophants: Constructions of Romantic Authority* (1991), *Allegories of One's Own Mind: Melancholy in Victorian Poetry* (2005), and the edited volume *Critical Essays on Dante Gabriel Rossetti* (1992).

We were not above raiding our own regional campuses. David Citino was brought back to Columbus, also in 1985; his appointment to the Marion campus in 1974 was mentioned in chapter 6. After a critical dissertation, he published a great many volumes of poetry. Among the most admired are those in the voice of Sister Mary Appassionata: *The Appassionata Poems* (1983), *The Appassionata Lectures* (1984), *The Appassionata Doctrines* (1986), and *The Book of Appassionata: Collected Poems* (1998). Other volumes include his first book, *Last Rites, and Other Poems* (1980); *The Gift of Fire* (1986); *The House of Memory* (1990); *The Discipline: New and Selected Poems, 1980–1992* (1992); *Broken Symmetry* (1997); *The Invention of Secrecy* (2001); *The News, and Other Poems* (2002); *Paperwork* (2003); and, posthumously, *A History of Hands* (2006). In prose, he co-authored the fifth edition of the study that John Gabel and Charles Wheeler had first brought out in 1986, *The Bible as Literature: An Introduction* (2005), and edited *The Eye of the Poet: Six Views of the Art and Craft of Poetry* (2002).

David was an especially beloved presence on campus; he was named Poet Laureate of the University, and he received the Alumni Award for Distinguished Teaching in 1981 and the Arts and Humanities Exemplary Faculty

FIGURE 8.3. David Citino

Award in 1992. He served for a time as director of the Creative Writing program, and as poetry editor of the Ohio State University Press. He was president of the Board of Trustees of the Thurber House. Among his many honors was the Ohio Humanities Council's Bjornson Award for Distinguished Service to the Humanities.

After a long and brave struggle with multiple sclerosis, David died in 2005.

Another external raid, and another one that brought a former Ph.D. student back home, was the appointment of Andrea Lunsford in 1986 (her Ph.D. had been awarded in 1977). Before returning, she published a revised edition of Dick Altick's *Preface to Critical Reading* in 1984.

Lunsford's account in chapter 5 of the OSU program in rhetoric and composition does not in fact do full justice to her own importance within that program, as an administrator and model and inspiration. She and Lisa Ede, who was a graduate student in the same years, have embodied their scholarly studies of the process of collaboration in writing, publishing together, for example, *Singular Texts/Plural Authors: Perspectives on Collaborative Writing* (1990) and *Writing Together: Collaboration in Theory and Practice, A Critical*

FIGURE 8.4. Andrea A. Lunsford

Sourcebook (2012). Other authors who were graduate students at the same time and with whom Andrea has published important work include Robert Connors (*The St. Martin's Handbook,* 1989); John J. Ruszkiewicz (*The Presence of Others: Readings for Critical Thinking and Writing,* 1994, and *Everything's an Argument,* 2001). With Ede and Connors she published a collection of essays in honor of Ed Corbett, *Essays on Classical Rhetoric and Modern Discourse* (1984)—and, with Ede, the *Selected Essays of Robert J. Connors* (2003). For the Modern Language Association she was one of the editors of *The Future of Doctoral Studies in English* (1989) and *The Right to Literacy* (1990); she also wrote the section on "Rhetoric and Composition" for the MLA's *Introduction to Scholarship in Modern Languages and Literatures* edited by Joseph Gibaldi (1992). Many of her publications have gone into several editions; other books include *Reclaiming Rhetorica: Women in the Rhetorical Tradition* (1995); *The Everyday Writer* (2002); *Crossing Borderlands: Composition and Postcolonial Studies* (2004); *Writing Matters: Rhetoric in Public and Private Lives* (2007, with Lisa Ede, Carole Clark Papper, and two other OSU colleagues, Beverly Moss and Keith Walters); and *Writing in Action* (2014).

A hint of Andrea's role as a mentor within the Department is contained in a note to the authors of the present history from Amy Shuman:

> Someone, I think the Director of Graduate Studies, was trying to set a time for some all-Department meetings. Whoever it was kept proposing different days at 5 pm, and Andrea kept saying she wasn't available then—and she needed to be at the meeting, whatever it was. Finally, someone asked her when she was available, and she said anytime, until the daycare center closed. Someone pointed out that she didn't have any children, and she said, "that's true, but the parents who do are untenured, and they can't complain about meeting after the daycare center closes, so I will." (I was already tenured then, and my children were older, so this didn't affect me—but it felt like a sea change.) From then on, our important meetings were during the day.[1]

In 2001, Andrea Lunsford left OSU for Stanford University, where she is the Louise Hewlett Nixon Professor of English Emerita. In 2002 she received the ADE Francis Andrew March Award from the MLA, honoring her distinguished service to the profession of English.

She continues to teach at the Bread Loaf School of English, and is a continuing presence and influence at Ohio State, where she has for a number of years been a member of the Department's English Advisory Committee. The newly renovated Graduate Student Lounge was named in her honor in 2018.

There were also several important appointments in 1986 that did not entail raids on other universities; three of them were connected in one way or another with twentieth-century literature. Mark Conroy was appointed in modernist literature, comparative literature, and the novel. His *Modernism and Authority: Strategies of Legitimation in Flaubert and Conrad* had appeared in 1985; he was promoted to Associate Professor in 1990. He was also the author of *Muse in the Machine: American Fiction and Mass Publicity* (2004). He was a member of the Board of Trustees of the Joseph Conrad Society. Mark died of cancer in 2018.

That same year, Jessica Prinz was appointed in modernist and postmodernist literature and interdisciplinary art. In addition to a number of essays on artists and writers, she has published *Art Discourse / Discourse in Art* (1991). She was promoted in 1992.

---

1. Amy Shuman, email, August 1, 2016.

FIGURE 8.5. Debra A. Moddelmog

Also in 1986 came the appointment of Debra A. Moddelmog, in twentieth-century American literature, multiculturalism, feminist theory, and gender studies. She was promoted to Associate Professor in 1992 and to Professor in 2001. She is the author of *Readers and Mythic Signs: The Oedipus Myth in Twentieth-Century Fiction* (1993) and *Reading Desire: In Pursuit of Ernest Hemingway* (1999); and co-editor of *Ernest Hemingway in Context* (2013) and *Samuel Steward and the Pursuit of the Erotic: Sexuality, Literature, Archives* (2017). As we have mentioned, she had coordinated a symposium, "Queer Places, Practices, and Places," in honor of Sam Steward in 2012. (On Sam Steward's career, see chapter 3.) By then Debra was the founder and Co-Director of the Sexuality Studies program and Co-Organizer and Director of the Diversity and Identity Studies Collective at OSU ("DISCO"). She served as Associate Dean in the College, and was appointed Chair of the English Department in 2014. She left OSU in 2016 to become Dean of the College of Liberal Arts at the University of Nevada, Reno.

At this point—and it's about time—we include the following account of the important and pervasive role of Women's Studies in the Department, by Valerie Lee.

WOMEN'S AND GENDER STUDIES

Valerie B. Lee

> Re-vision—the act of looking back, of seeing with fresh eyes, of
> entering an old text from a new critical direction—is for women
> more than a chapter in cultural history: it is an act of survival.
> —Adrienne Rich, "When We Dead Awaken: Writing as Re-Vision" (1971)

In 1952 when Robert Mason Myers comically recast the literary canon as *From Beowulf to Virginia Woolf*, he probably had little idea that so many women authors in addition to Woolf would one day demand rooms of their own. Twenty years after the publication of Myers's book, feminism knocked on the doors of the literary canon, eager to challenge reading lists, the curriculum, and departmental politics. The Vietnam War, the Civil Rights Movement, and widespread social unrest fomented changes, especially in the academy. Awakened by Betty Friedan's *Feminine Mystique* (1963), which asserted that heretofore there were "problems that had no name," and emboldened by Kate Millett's *Sexual Politics* (1970), which denounced the works of D. H. Lawrence, Henry Miller, Norman Mailer, and other male authors for their patriarchal, sexist viewpoints, Second-Wave feminists found literature departments ripe candidates for "consciousness raising."[2] If Emily Dickinson and Virginia Woolf could be in the canon, then why not Kate Chopin, Eudora Welty, Doris Lessing, Adrienne Rich, and Sylvia Plath? And if the aforementioned white women authors were added, why not also Zora Neale Hurston, Alice Walker, Toni Cade Bambara, Toni Morrison, Bharati Mukherjee, Louise Erdrich, Leslie Marmon Silko, Maxine Hong Kingston, Amy Tan, Joy Harjo, Ana Castillo, Julia Alvarez, Sandra Cisneros, and many others?

Because the early days of Feminist Studies were so closely aligned with literature departments, it is not surprising that persons in the Department of English at The Ohio State University were at the forefront of what later would become a strong presence of women's and gender studies on campus, culminating in a Department of Women's, Gender and Sexuality Studies. Today's Department of English has many women professors and women authors and theorists who infuse the curriculum. An early pioneer with strong feminist sensibilities was English Department professor Mildred Brand Munday. In *Sojourner*, the then Women's Studies Newsletter, Munday recalls the "joy and incredulity" of the 1970s: "Bricks were thrown, mimeograph machines ran overtime, tear gas was plentifully released, *agents provocateurs* from the Columbus police appeared on campus,

---

2. This is shorthand for understanding why and how established authorities, typically white and male, wield their power in policing gender, race, class, sexual identity, and other categories of difference.

and fuzzy-cheeked National Guardsmen lurked around corners with loaded rifles and sharpened bayonets." In this essay titled "Affirmative (?) Action (?)," Munday reminds readers of what had happened at Kent State and of the irony that the events on Ohio State's campus were occurring in its centenary year. She takes hope, however, in the changes on campus as a result of the turbulent decade: the formation of an Office of Women's Studies and a Department of English welcoming her Women's Literature specialty as readily as it welcomed her Shakespearean Studies specialty. Munday's influence was such that posthumously the Department of Women's, Gender and Sexuality Studies created a scholarship in her honor that provides $3,000 for tuition (https://wgss.osu.edu/undergraduate/mildred-munday-scholarship).

Whereas one might have suspected that Munday, a graduate of two women's colleges, Randolph-Macon College and Smith College, would be at the helm of a campus feminist movement, the sustained and fervent activism of two other English professors, Barbara Rigney and Marlene Longenecker, might have taken some by surprise. In the early 1970s Barbara Rigney joined Verta Taylor (Sociology) and Leila Rupp (History) to secretly form an ad-hoc women's studies committee that went public only after the committee had completed a 30-page proposal "outlining the desirability, viability, and structure for a Center of Women's Studies."[3] As some of the earliest teachers of what would become "Women in Literature," Rigney and graduate students such as Pamela Transue taught women writers as part of the Comparative Studies program. Later in her career Transue would become President of Tacoma Community College, and Rigney would publish several well-received books on women authors and thinkers: *The Voices of Toni Morrison*; *Madness and Sexual Politics in the Feminist Novel*; *Margaret Atwood*; and *Lilith's Daughters: Women and Religion in Contemporary Fiction*.

Storming out of Santa Monica, California, and taking seriously Laurel Thatcher Ulrich's off-quoted feminist quip, "Well-behaved women seldom make history,"[4] was the other feminist activist in the Ohio State Department of English: Marlene Longenecker. There was no doubt that she was truly a product of the sixties and seventies: long scarves, Birkenstock shoes, peace symbol necklaces, mother to many

---

3. This history was shared on May 1, 2015 at the fortieth anniversary celebration of the Department of Women's, Gender and Sexuality Studies and is a part of the historical archives of that department. An oral presentation of this material and event is on the Department's website: https://wgss.osu.edu/40th-anniversary-celebration.

4. Harvard historian Ulrich used this phrase in a scholarly article in 1976, and it fast became a slogan in the women's movement. Later Ulrich would publish *Well-Behaved Women Seldom Make History*, Alfred A. Knopf, 2007.

cats,[5] and Longenecker had actually lived in a commune. Very active in NWSA [the National Women's Studies Association], Longenecker unabashedly fought for women's rights and took on enough administrative appointments to dilute male-dominated Departmental politics. As Graduate Studies Chair, Vice Chair, departmental scheduler, and tireless committee member, Longenecker's influence on the everyday life and lore of the department was widespread. As a two-time recipient of the university's Alumni Award for Distinguished Teaching, Longenecker taught feminist theory with the same energy that suffragettes pursued the vote.

Today, there are many English professors who hold affiliated status with the University's current Department of Women's, Gender and Sexuality Studies: Jian Chen (Gender and Sexuality Studies and Asian American and Asian Diasporas); Wendy Hesford (Gender and Sexuality Studies and Human Rights Rhetoric); Lynn Itagaki (Women of Color Feminisms and Interracial Ethics); Nan Johnson (Rhetoric and Gender); Debra Moddelmog (Gender and Sexuality Studies and twentieth-century American Literature); Cynthia L. Selfe (Literacy Studies and Digital Media Studies); and Amy Shuman (Gender and Sexuality Studies and Folklore). Several others have gender and sexuality as strengths that complement their disciplinary areas but do not have a formal appointment with the Department of Women's, Gender and Sexuality Studies, including Sandra Macpherson, Roxann Wheeler, and Elizabeth Kolkovich.

Whenever one is engaged in "subverting hegemonic discourses," as we feminists are fond of describing our work, that work becomes expansive and inclusive. Beyond adding "Women in Literature courses," the Department began offering courses in queer studies and queer theory as a lens for analyses. Literary, visual, and rhetorical representations of the political diversity of straight, lesbian, bisexual, queer, and transgender communities became important, as well as fields such as (Dis)ability Studies. Additionally, globalization and geopolitical identities stretched the boundaries of what historically had been American and British Literature. Against this larger backdrop of acknowledging that all categories of identity mutually inform and constitute each other, the Department of English hired professors who were very intentional in producing scholarship and teaching courses on the representation of sexualities, nationally and internationally. Among this group of professors were Thomas Piontek, Andrea Newlyn, Norman Jones, Martin Joseph Ponce, and Jian Chen. The undergraduate curriculum added

---

5. One of the best descriptions of Longenecker's life is the obituary written by Susan Williams for *The Columbus Dispatch*, February 8, 2016. Williams writes that Longenecker "adjusted herself to life in the Midwest by surrounding herself with an ever expanding collection of books, baskets, jewelry, Birkenstocks, crafts, Democratic political pins and bumper stickers, and treasures from her numerous trips to England."

such courses as "Special Topics in LGBTQ Literature and Culture" and "Introduction to Queer Studies." At the graduate level, in addition to English 7890:
"Seminar in Feminist Studies in Literature and Culture," the upper-level Seminar in Critical Theory can have a queer, feminist, and/or intersectionality focus;
and feminist and queer approaches are options for the Contemporary Movements
course. These courses proved popular with graduate students. The list of students
producing dissertations in the field of Women's and Gender Studies is very long,
driven by student interest and their preparation for diverse careers.

The personal is political.
—Second Wave Feminism slogan

Although I was a graduate student in the Department of English in the 1970s,
I have no memory of women teaching graduate courses, as most were assistant
professors and not senior professors. Perhaps there was such a woman teaching
rhetoric and composition courses, but not doctoral-level literature courses. When
I returned to campus in the 1990s as a senior professor—fresh from a campus that
required the first general education course in Women's and Black Studies and still
reeling from provocative lectures by ardent feminist pioneers Flo Kennedy, Flor-
ence Howe, and Catherine Stimpson—I greatly appreciated the fact that English
professors at Ohio State were teaching a robust list of women authors and theorists. As someone who had already been attending a number of women's studies
conferences and armed with T-shirts that announced, "Transforming the Academy," I was particularly honored to work alongside Marlene, who had a national
reputation in feminist studies. When the NWSA was held in the early 80s on the
Ohio State campus, I attended partly because I had my first baby and full-time
child care was provided, but also because I knew that many professors in the Ohio
State Department of English were on the program, including, of course, Marlene,
director of the Women's Studies Center (1980–86). The only blip to Ohio's hosting of the national organization would occur a few years later in Akron when
racial politics shredded the success of the conference. One of the NWSA founding members, Barbara W. Gerber, notes that the conference attendees threw out
Robert's Rules of Order for a fictional Roberta's Rules of Order, and in one of
her essay's sub-headings, "Rising from the Ashes," she names Marlene as someone
who helped salvage the spirit and substance of the organization.[6] Marlene would
later share with me that the Akron conference dampened the spirits of many of
the attendees, some of whom forever left the organization. Although Marlene

6. "Rising from the Ashes" is one of the sub-titles in Gerber's longer essay, "NWSA Organizational Development: A View from Within, at 25 Years," *NWSA Journal* 14.1 (2002): 1–21.
Gerber describes the set of events as a critical situation wherein she, Marlene, and five other
committee members "were urged to proceed with appropriate caution and haste" (16).

continued working on the national level, she concentrated on galvanizing coalitions and allies for women's interests and feminist studies at the Departmental and University levels.

By the 1990s, a large number of male and female professors in the Department of English included women authors and critics in their course offerings. On the day of my job talk, I remember walking with Jeredith Merrin and Debra Moddlemog across the Oval to the Faculty Club and hearing the fascinating work that they were doing in feminist and gender studies. Although the Department still did not have more than one or two women full professors, there were many women associate professors and assistant professors, representing a range of feminist sensibilities. I was most interested in the agenda of black feminist thought, with its heavy emphases on intersectionality—the intersections of gender, race, class, sexuality, ethnicity, and nationality. With my hire, the hiring of Lynda Zwinger, a specialist in feminist theory and nineteenth-century American Studies, and the hiring of Leigh Gilmore, the English Department was entering an era of jointly appointed professors with Women's Studies. Much to my chagrin, Lynda returned to her previous institution, the University of Arizona, and Leigh switched her whole appointment to English, greatly fortifying feminist theory, trauma studies, and autobiographical studies within that Department. Eventually, Leigh accepted a job at Scripps College, but not before hosting symposia, teaching a wide range of classes, and giving lectures that deepened conversations on gender and social justice and the politics of representation.

In general, the history of women and gender studies in English is interconnected with the history of the University's Women's, Gender and Sexuality department, and my disadvantage in telling such a story is that I have always been between and betwixt the two units. I ended up chairing both at different times. For me, it was a seamless stretch, and now trying to separate the historical threads is difficult. Compounding that intertwined history is that another full professor in English, Linda Mizejewski, chaired Women's Studies and moved 100% of her appointment to that unit. Linda had been instrumental in developing courses in English on feminist film theory and popular culture.

My personal recollection of Women's and Gender Studies in the Ohio State Department of English came to full satisfaction when I had the honor of hiring an Arts and Humanities Distinguished Professor in the Humanities, another West Coast woman willing to settle in the Midwest. Hailing from California with the same feminist confidence and social justice agenda as Marlene, this hire, Robyn Warhol, strengthened the department's emphases in feminist theory, nineteenth-century women's writings, and narrative theory. Robyn authored *Gendered Interventions: Narrative Discourse in the Victorian Novel* (Rutgers UP, 1989), which lays out an early justification for feminist narratology and develops the notion of the "engaging narrator" in feminine nineteenth-century texts; and *Having a Good Cry: Effeminate Feelings and Popular Forms* (Ohio State UP, 2003), a study of the ways sentimental, romantic, and serial texts work to establish and reinforce gendered performance in fans of TV, Hollywood film, and fiction. With Diane Price-Herndl, she co-edited *Feminisms: An Anthology of Literary Theory and Criticism* (Rutgers UP, 1991, 1997). One of my personal joys has been working with Robyn on the national level for the Association of Departments of English (ADE), where we both served as Presidents and crafted a series of guidelines for Departments of English wishing to increase diversity. Whereas Mildred Munday's 1970 plea in *Sojourner,* "Affirmative (?) Action (?)," questioned whether departments had the will to push a diversity agenda, Robyn would boldly tweak the title of our ADE document from a hesitant "Affirmative Action" to a decisive "Affirmative Activism."

One often hears those who major or minor with concentrations in Women's and Gender Studies speak of how these fields "saved their lives." I am not about to go that far, but I do happily acknowledge that gender and race have shaped my theories, methodologies, and construction of myself in the academy. Moreover, I am indebted to the Department of English, a department that has been expansive without losing focus, accommodating without losing integrity, progressive without losing traditions. In such a climate, Women's and Gender Studies can expect to continue thriving.

Works Cited

Friedan, Betty. *The Feminine Mystique.* W. W. Norton, 1963.

Gerber, Barbara W. "NWSA Organizational Development: A View from Within, at 25 Years." *NWSA Journal* 14.1 (Spring 2002): 1–21.

Hubbard, Dolan, and Paula Krebs, David Laurence, Valerie Lee, Doug Steward, and Robyn Warhol. "Affirmative Activism: Report of the ADE Ad Hoc Committee on the Status of African American Faculty Members in English." *ADE Bulletin* (Winter-Spring 2007): 70–74.

Millett, Kate. *Sexual Politics.* Doubleday, 1970.

Munday, Mildred B. "Affirmative (?) Action (?)." Guest Editorial, *Sojourner.* Office of Women's Studies, The Ohio State University, VI, No. 2 (October 1979).

Myers, Robert Mason. *From Beowulf to Virginia Woolf: An Astonishing and Wholly Unauthorized History of English Literature.* Bobbs-Merrill, 1952.

Valerie mentions the ADE; the first national meeting (or "Summer Seminar") of the Association of Departments of English—a group composed chiefly of chairs of English departments—to be held at OSU took place in July

1986. David Frantz was Vice Chair, and through his friendship with Howard D. and Babette Sirak, all the visiting chairs were able one afternoon to visit the Sirak home, which still contained the magnificent art collection that the Siraks would later donate to the Columbus Museum of Art.

Around this time, David also took on the responsibility of directing the entire program in Rhetoric and Composition. There had been for some time a problem of morale entailing a perceived "split" between those primarily involved in the language and writing programs and everyone else. The composition staff, for example, sometimes felt that not enough attention was paid to their role, a feeling that was sometimes felt, as well, by those whose chief interests were literary. David was an ideal administrator to confront the resulting controversies and tensions, and the appointment of Andrea and others also helped to lessen those problems.

After doing a great deal to resolve those issues, David was appointed by Dean Micheal Riley of the College of Humanities to be Associate Dean. Arnold Shapiro took over as Vice Chair. Arnie had already been heading the New Personnel Committee, which entailed not only searching for new faculty but recruiting them as well. It was an era when faculty positions were scarce across the nation, but even so the Department of course had to compete for the most promising candidates.

With Beja curtailing his teaching, another appointment in modern literature was made in 1987, of Sebastian D. G. Knowles (promoted in 1992 and in 2001). He is the author of *A Purgatorial Flame: Seven British Writers in The Second World War* (1990); *An Annotated Bibliography of a Decade of T. S. Eliot Criticism, 1977–1986* (1992); and *At Fault: Joyce and the Crisis of the Modern University* (2018). His *Dublin Helix: The Life of Language in Joyce's Ulysses* (2001) won the Michael J. Durkan Prize for Books on Language and Culture sponsored by the American Conference for Irish Studies. He is the editor of *Bronze by Gold: The Music of Joyce* (1999) and *Joyce in Trieste: An Album of Risky Readings* (2007). Seb is on the Board of Editors of the *James Joyce Quarterly*, and is the General Series Editor of the Florida James Joyce Series, of the University Press of Florida.

Knowles received the Arts and Sciences Outstanding Teaching Award, in 2000, was named the English Graduate Professor of the Year in 2000, was given the College of Humanities Rodica C. Botoman Award for Distinguished Undergraduate Teaching and Mentoring in 2003, and was named English Undergraduate Professor of the Year in 2007. He was a Fulbright Lecturer at the University of Antwerp, where he was named Arts Professor of the Year in 2005.

Sebastian was the President of the International James Joyce Foundation from 2012 to 2016. The Foundation had been brought to Ohio State in 1989,

FIGURE 8.6. Sebastian D. G. Knowles

during Murray Beja's term as its President; it stayed at OSU (with Beja as the Executive Secretary) until 2017, when it moved to the University of Tulsa, where it had started in 1967.

Also indirectly because of Beja's curtailed teaching, two prominent people in Irish studies were brought to the Department as visitors in the early nineties: Deirdre Bair, the biographer of Samuel Beckett as well as of Simone de Beauvoir, Carl Jung, and Anaïs Nin; and Richard Finneran, critic and editor of William Butler Yeats.

Meanwhile, appointments in other fields were also being made. Audrey Jaffe came to OSU in 1987, in Victorian literature and narrative theory. She is the author of *Vanishing Points: Dickens, Narrative, and the Subject of Omniscience* (1991) and *Scenes of Sympathy: Identity and Representation in Victorian Fiction* (2000); and, after she left OSU for the University of Toronto (we could still be raided), *The Affective Life of the Average Man: The Victorian Novel and the Stock-Market Graph* (2010) and *The Victorian Novel Dreams of the Real: Conventions and Ideology* (2016).

H. Lewis Ulman (Louie) was also hired in 1987, in Rhetoric and Composition with special interests in nature writing, eighteenth-century philosophy, and computers and literacy. He is the author of *Things, Thoughts, Words, and Actions: The Problem of Language in Late Eighteenth-Century British Rhetorical Theory* (1994) and the editor of *The Minutes of the Aberdeen Philosophical Society, 1758–1773* (1990). With his colleagues Scott De Witt and Cynthia Selfe he edited *Stories That Speak to Us: Exhibits from the Digital Archive of Literacy Narratives* (2013). He was promoted to Associate Professor in 1993 and served a stint as Vice Chair for Rhetoric and Composition. Louie retired in 2014.

During these years, when the number of positions for persons with graduate degrees in English had been declining for some time, the Department decided to decrease the number of graduate students in its program, though gradually rather than drastically. It also removed the required status of the bibliography course, English 980, making it an elective in 1988.

One innovation was the first Graduate Student Conference, sponsored by and for graduate students here and nationally. As Jim Phelan reflected in his diary notes at the time, "The conference, I think, has energized a lot of us. It's been a very impressive affair, one that Jamie [Barlowe-Kayes], Pat [Sullivan], Cheryl [Glenn], Amy [Goodwin] and the others who put it together should be very proud of. My counterparts and I at Chicago would never have dreamed of doing anything like this. The conference's success has inspired some students at Wisconsin-Milwaukee to commit themselves to organizing something similar next year."[7] In fact, other graduate students from elsewhere as well took up the challenge, and the result was a series of such conferences. OSU again hosted one—the fifth—in 1991. Much of the source of that success surely had to do with the perspective that graduate students brought to such get-togethers, not so much because of age, perhaps, as because of their role within the profession and the discipline.

We should mention here that a reader who wishes to get a sense of what it was like to be a member of the Department in the 1980s (and beyond, for that matter), could well read Phelan's *Beyond the Tenure Track*. One would learn a good deal about what a faculty member does, and feels, how difficult and worrisome being an advisor of graduate students can be; and how challenging and frustrating (and gratifying) teaching can be; and the roles in the life of a faculty member of research, and writing, and "service." Along the way, one gets a realistic and sometimes sobering picture of academic "politics"—but of collegiality as well.

Informing faculty members of the results of tenure and promotion decisions can be among the most rewarding, or heart-wrenching, of a Chair's responsibilities. As we have said, we have chosen in this history not to dwell

7. Phelan, *Beyond the Tenure Track*, 154.

on the unfortunate instances when faculty members did not achieve tenure. When that happens, somehow, at some point, for some reason, the process has failed. It is a common saying among Chairs that it is when one has to tell a candidate that the senior faculty has decided against tenure that the Chairs "earn their money." We are mentioning one case now because of its unusual drama.

Thomas Murray, a linguist, had been appointed as an Assistant Professor in 1983 by Julian Markels. He did not make it through the fourth-year review in 1987. Understandably, he was very disturbed; when Morris Beja had to inform him about the decision, he was angrier than anyone Beja ever had to confront on such an occasion. Tom Murray came to Sara Garnes's office after the decision, believing that she had provided a negative report on his scholarship, and told her that she would be glad to hear that "I've decided not to slash your tires."

In 1985, Tom married Carmin Ross, who had taken one of his classes the previous year. She graduated with a major in English and obtained a degree in law from OSU. In 1988 she went with Tom to Manhattan, Kansas, where he had obtained a faculty appointment at Kansas State University. They had a daughter, and when they divorced there was a custody battle. In 2003, when the daughter was four years old, Carmin Ross was found brutally murdered; in 2005, Tom Murray was convicted of first-degree murder. (Among the voluminous evidence was the fact that he was found to have conducted Internet searches on "how to murder someone and not get caught."[8]) Beja had come to realize that he had told someone who would be legally deemed capable of murder that he was fired.

On to much happier outcomes.

Michelle Herman was hired in Creative Writing in 1988 (and promoted to Associate Professor in 1994 and to Professor in 2006). She is the author of the novels *Missing* (1990), *Dog* (2005), and *Devotion* (2016), the collection of novellas *A New and Glorious Life* (1998), and the essay collections *The Middle of Everything: Memoirs of Motherhood* (2005), *Stories We Tell Ourselves* (2013), and *Like a Song* (2015), as well as a book for children, *A Girl's Guide to Life* (2015). Her honors include a National Endowment for the Arts Fellowship, a James Michener Fellowship, fellowships from the Ohio Arts Council and the Greater Columbus Arts Council, and, from OSU, the University Alumni Distinguished Teaching Award and the Rodica C. Botoman Award for Distinguished Undergraduate Teaching and Mentoring. She has been the Director of

---

8. Ian Cummings, "Court rejects convicted murderer Thomas Murray's challenge of prison sentence," *Lawrence Journal-World*, April 11, 2013 (http://www2.ljworld.com/news/2013/apr/11/court-rejects-convicted-murderer-thomas-murrays-ch/).

FIGURE 8.7. Michelle Herman

the Creative Writing program and also directs the Graduate Interdisciplinary Specialization in Fine Arts and a summer program for teenage writers, the Young Writers Workshop.

Kitty Locker came to OSU as an Assistant Professor in Rhetoric and Composition in 1988 with a specialty in business and professional writing. She was promoted in 1990. She was the author of *Business and Administrative Communication* (1995) and the co-author of *Business Communication: Building Critical Skills* (1994), and served as the editor of the *Journal of Business Communication* and as President of the Association for Business Communication. Kitty died in 2006. The Department has several awards in business and professional writing in her name: the Kitty Locker Prize for Excellence in Business Communication; the Kitty O. Locker Travel Awards; and the Kitty O. Locker Undergraduate Professional Writing Contest.

Jeredith Merrin (hired in 1988 and promoted in 1993 and 1997) was appointed in the area of twentieth-century poetry and published *An Enabling Humility: Marianne Moore, Elizabeth Bishop, and the Uses of Tradition* in 1990. She continued publishing critical essays, but her career turned more and more to writing her own poetry, including the collections *Shift* (1996) and *Bat Ode* (2001).

FIGURE 8.8. Beverly Moss

Also hired in 1988 was Beverly Moss, in the fields of composition and literacy studies; she was promoted to Associate Professor in 1995. Her *A Community Text Arises: A Literate Text and a Literate Tradition in African-American Churches* appeared in 2003. With Andrea Lunsford, Michal Brody, Lisa Ede, Carole Clark Papper, and Keith Walters, she is the author of *Everyone's an Author* (2012). She has also edited *Writing Groups inside and outside the Classroom,* with Nels Highberg and Melissa Nicolas (2004) and *The Best of the Independent Journals in Rhetoric and Composition 2012,* with Julia Voss, Steve Parks, Brian Baille, Steph Ceraso, and Heather Christiansen (2014). She received the University Alumni Award for Distinguished Teaching in 2018.

In other developments around this time, the English Department gained its Commons Room, when the University—in return for the space occupied by the English Department Library in Derby Hall—agreed to renovate two classrooms, Denney 311 and 313, thus providing a venue for Department meetings, lectures, and receptions.

Also in the mid- to late eighties, the College of Humanities began to provide all tenure-track faculty with computers. Gradually, too, the faculty and staff introduced themselves to email (although for a while, among some faculty, not without some suspicion that the College and the University might use the system to spy on their correspondence).

Several important appointments were made in 1989. John King, a scholar of Renaissance literature, was hired as a full Professor from Bates College; he became Distinguished University Professor. In addition to a Guggenheim Fellowship (2009), he has received fellowships from the American Council of Learned Societies, the American Philosophical Society, the Bibliographical Society of America, the Folger Shakespeare Library, the Huntington Library, the National Endowment for the Humanities, the Renaissance Society of America, and the Rockefeller Foundation. Among his books are *English Reformation Literature: The Tudor Origins of the Protestant Tradition* (1982); *Tudor Royal Iconography: Literature and Art in an Age of Religious Crisis* (1989); *Spenser's Poetry and the Reformation Tradition* (1990); *Milton and Religious Controversy: Satire and Polemic in "Paradise Lost"* (2000); and *Foxe's "Book of Martyrs" and Early Modern Print Culture* (2006). He has also edited a number of other books, including *John Foxe and His World* (2002) with his colleague, Christopher Highley.

Roger Cherry was hired in the field of composition, rhetorical theory and the history of rhetoric also in 1989. He is the author of *A Brief Guide to Basic Writing* (1993) and co-editor of *A Rhetoric of Doing: Essays on Written Discourse in Honor of James L. Kinneavy* (1992, with Stephen P. Witte and Neil Nakadate).

Frank Donoghue was hired as an eighteenth-century scholar that same year and published *The Fame Machine: Book Reviewing and Eighteenth-Century Literary Careers* in 1996. He has gone on to a special interest in the study of the history and future of higher education, especially of the humanities, in the United States, as in *The Last Professors: The Corporate University and the Fate of the Humanities* (2008).

He was promoted to Associate Professor in 1995 and to Professor in 2011.

The choice of the Nancy Dasher Award by the CEAO in creative writing to Lee K. Abbott of Case Western University helped the Department to know about his fine work in fiction, and so a raid on Case Western brought Abbott to OSU as a Professor in 1989. He had already published in 1986 both *Love Is the Crooked Thing: Stories* and *Strangers in Paradise*. Among his many other collections of short fiction are *Dreams of Distant Lives: Stories* (1989, the year he came to OSU); *Living after Midnight* (1991); *Wet Places at Noon* (1997); *All Things, All at Once: New and Selected Stories* (2006); and *One of Star Wars One of Doom* (2007). Lee died after a bout with cancer in 2019.

Kathy Fagan (Kathy Fagan Grandinetti), also hired in Creative Writing in 1989, is the author of the poetry collections *The Raft* (1985); *MOVING & ST*

RAGE (1999); *The Charm* (2002); and *Lip* (2009). She has received fellowships from the NEA, the Ingram Merrill Foundation, the Frost Place, and the Ohio Arts Council. She is the Director of Creative Writing and Series Editor for the OSU Press/*The Journal* Wheeler Poetry Prize. In 2017 the Columbus Foundation presented her with the Raymond J. Hanley Award of $12,500, given to an artist who has demonstrated a high level of achievement for at least five years. She received promotions in 1994 and 2002.

In 1990, Nan Johnson was hired as an Associate Professor in the history and theory of composition and rhetoric. She was promoted to Professor in 2002. Nan is the author of *Nineteenth-Century Rhetoric in North America* (1991) and *Gender and Rhetorical Space in American Life, 1866–1910* (2002).

That same year Kay Halasek was also hired in rhetorical and composition theory and history. She is the author of *A Pedagogy of Possibility: Bakhtinian Perspectives on Composition Studies* (1999) and co-editor of *Writing Lives: Reading Communities* (2000) and *Landmark Essays on Basic Writing* (2001). Kay currently directs the University Institute for Teaching and Learning.

Clare Simmons was hired in nineteenth-century British literature in 1990, the same year she published *Reversing the Conquest: History and Myth in Nineteenth-Century British Literature*; she was promoted in 1996 and 2000. She is also the author of *Eyes across the Channel: French Revolutions, Party History and British Writing, 1830–1882* (2000) and *Popular Medievalism in Romantic-Era Britain* (2011), and editor of Charlotte M. Yonge's *Clever Woman of the Family* and *Medievalism and the Quest for the "Real" Middle Ages* (both 2001). She is also the editor of *Prose Studies*.

Clare is currently the Director of Undergraduate Studies. In the 1980s there was a vast increase in the number of undergraduate English majors. The Self-Study report of 1978 had lamented the difficulty of attracting majors; by 1991, in his retirement message, "Hail and Farewell," Arnie Shapiro wrote that "For the past several years I've been very worried about increasing enrollments (our problem is exactly the reverse of the central concern expressed in our self-study of ten years ago; then we worried that we had too few English majors, now we have too many) and closed courses."[9] In the Spring of 1992, Marlene Longenecker reported that the number of majors had gone from 190 in 1980 to 845.

The increase came about because of a number of factors, including the fact that around this time the College of Education did away with its undergraduate English major, and the Department of Communication severely limited

_____

9. *Impromptu* 9.1 (Autumn 1991): 2.

FIGURE 8.9. Kay Halasek

its enrollment. The new numbers in any case arose in spite of (or because of?) the fact that the major had become more rigorous and demanding. The Department had gone from requiring fifty course credits for the major to sixty. As Marlene said, the additional ten hours were added at the upper levels: "In the 35 hours of upper division work, students must take courses in: *at least* two historical periods (e.g., the Renaissance and the nineteenth century) and *at least* two of the following areas of English studies: literature, film, folklore, writing and rhetoric, creative writing, language, and critical theory. In addition, the 35 hours will include a minimum of 15 hours in a Focus Area to be determined by the student and his or her adviser. This Focus Area is where the students will concentrate their special interests; it can be centered in the traditional canon, or it can be very interdisciplinary; it can focus on writing or on reading, on film or on fiction, on a theme or a period or a genre."[10]

The enrollments helped the Department make a case for a significant number of faculty appointments in 1991. Nicholas Howe was attracted from

---

10. *Impromptu* 9.2 (Spring 1992): 2.

the University of Oklahoma as an Associate Professor in medieval literature, and was promoted to full Professor in 1995. He served as the Director of the Center for Medieval and Renaissance Studies from that year until he left for the University of California, Berkeley in 2002. Before arriving at Ohio State he had published *The Old English Catalogue Poems: A Study in Poetic Form* (1985) and *Migration and Mythmaking in Anglo-Saxon England* (1989). Then came *Across an Inland Sea: Writing in Place from Buffalo to Berlin* (2003); *Home and Homelessness in the Medieval and Renaissance World* (2004); and *Writing the Map of Anglo-Saxon England: Essays in Cultural Geography* (2007). He edited *A Critic's Notebook,* by his father, the eminent critic Irving Howe, in 1994. Like Kitty Locker, Nick died prematurely; he was a victim, in his fifties, of leukemia, a few years after joining the faculty at Berkeley.

Another person who died early was Jon Erickson, in his early sixties, in 2016. He was appointed as an Assistant Professor in 1991 in drama and critical theory, and was a gifted performance artist and poet. His *Fate of the Object: From Modern Object to Postmodern Sign in Performance, Art, and Poetry* appeared in 1995. He was promoted to Associate Professor in 1996.

Chris Highley was also appointed in 1991, in early modern literature and culture. He was promoted to Associate Professor in 1997, the year his *Shakespeare, Spenser, and the Crisis in Ireland* appeared, and to full Professor in 2009. He is also the author of *Catholics Writing the Nation in Early Modern Britain and Ireland* (2008) and, with John King, has edited *John Foxe and His World* (2002) and *Henry VIII and His Afterlives: Literature, Politics, and Art* (2009).

OSU raided Denison University in 1991 to bring back Valerie Lee, who as Valerie Gray had written a 1976 dissertation, on Ralph Ellison and Herman Melville, directed by Julian Markels. She came as an Associate Professor in American literature, African American literature, Folklore, and Gender and Sexuality Studies, and was promoted to full in 1998. She is the author of *Granny Midwives and Black Women Writers: Double-Dutched Readings* (1996) and editor of *The Prentice Hall Anthology of African American Women's Literature* (2006). She received the University Alumni Award for Distinguished Teaching in 1993 and the University Faculty Award for Distinguished University Service in 2006.

Valerie became the first African American and the first woman to chair the Department of English, in 2002 (see the Epilogue to this history). She went on as well to become the Vice President for Outreach and Engagement, the Vice Provost for Diversity and Inclusion, and the chief Diversity Officer for the University, and also chaired the Departments of Women' Studies

FIGURE 8.10. Valerie Lee

(and then Women's, Gender, and Sexuality Studies) and African American and African Studies.

We have provided above Valerie's account of Women's and Gender Studies in the Department; it's with gratitude that we present here her account of the role of African American literature, one that tells a great deal about the entire profession as well as the Department of English at Ohio State.

AFRICAN AMERICAN LITERATURE IN OHIO STATE'S DEPARTMENT OF ENGLISH

Valerie Lee

I wrote my first novel because I wanted to read it.
—Toni Morrison

I want to share two histories: first, a rather formal one that future scholars and administrators might browse for factual details, and second, a history from the perspective of a twenty-three-year-old African American graduate student who walked into Denney Hall to register for classes on a hot day in August 1973 and who twenty-nine years later would chair that department.

The Formal History

The Ohio State University Department of English doctoral graduate studies program propelled the careers of several nationally known African Americanists, including: Charles Henry Rowell (class of 1972), founder and editor of one of the field's leading and longest running literary magazines, *Callaloo: A Journal of African Diaspora Arts and Letters*; Trudier Harris (class of 1973), currently University Distinguished Research Professor, Department of English, the University of Alabama, and, formerly, longtime holder of the J. Carlyle Sitterson Professor of English Chair at the University of North Carolina, Chapel Hill, and author of dozens of books on African American Women's Literature, Black Southern Literature, and Black Cultural and Folkloric Studies; John W. Roberts (class of 1976), fellow and past president of the American Folklore Society, chair of the Afro-American Studies program at the University of Pennsylvania and the African and African American Studies Department at The Ohio State University, Dean of Humanities and Liberal Arts and Social Sciences at Ohio State and the University of Houston respectively, and the Clinton White House Deputy Chairman of the National Endowment for the Humanities; Valerie B. Lee (class of 1976), African American Women's Literature and Folklore, former chair of two Ohio State departments—Women's Studies and English—a past president of ADE (Association of Departments of English), and an Ohio State Vice Provost and Vice President; and Sally Ann H. Ferguson (class of 1978), University of North Carolina, Greensboro, specialist on African American authors, most notably Charles W. Chesnutt, and a past president of MELUS (The Society for the Study of Multiethnic Literature of the US).

There are reasons why many of these notable graduates are from the same era and have specialties in African American Folklore. They took advantage of the Department's reputation as home to nationally recognized folklorists. Among this group of folklorists was Professor Patrick Mullen, who, well aware of the connection between African American Literature and its folkloric roots, intersections, and themes, mentored Harris, Roberts, Lee, Ferguson, and others who became scholars of African American Literature.

As with most departments of English nationwide, the Ohio State Department of English began to strengthen African American Literature as a result of literary canon wars spanning the 1980s and 1990s. Prior to this time period, if African American authors were taught at all, those taught were the male trinity: Richard Wright, James Baldwin, and Ralph Ellison. As a nod to growing feminist sensibilities, some professors added Gwendolyn Brooks. But for the most part, African American Literature had to prove and claim its right to status in the academy. During the 1970s those seeking courses in Black Diaspora Literature were most likely to find such courses down the street from Denney Hall, in University Hall, where the department of Black Studies (now African American and African Studies) was located. Sprinkled throughout the next two decades a second cohort of students in the Department of English wrote dissertations on African American Literature and or Folklore and began long-term university careers, including: Fayetteville State professor and a former president of the College Language Association, Booker T. Anthony (class of 1988); Jackson State University professor Wanda Macon Morgan (class of 1992); Fayetteville State University professor Brooksie Harrington (class of 1992), whose scholarly work on gospel singer Shirley Caesar is housed at Harlem's Schomburg Library; Florida International University professor Alfonso Hawkins Jr. (class of 1993 and author of *The Jazz Trope: A Theory of African American Literary and Vernacular Culture*); Andrews University professor Joseph Warren, who started in Ohio State's graduate program in the early 70s and returned in the 90s for his dissertation defense.

Slower than the growth of producing graduates of color has been the hiring of professors specializing in African American Literature. When Professor Beverly Moss was hired in 1988 as a newly minted Ph.D. with a specialty in composition and community literacy practices, she also was tapped to teach English 281: Introduction to African American Literature. Before accepting appointments at other institutions, Professor John Stewart served a stint teaching folklore and African American Literature, as did Roland Williams, Jr., and Rolland Murray. As a field, African American Literature could not accommodate a sequence of undergraduate and graduate courses until alumni professors Lee and Roberts returned to the Department. With their return and the return of Jacqueline Jones Royster, who had an earlier stint as a visiting professor, the senior presence of African Americans increased, enhancing the many persons in the Department whose scholarship already had a stake in African American Studies. Indeed, by the year 2000 the number of faculty doing African American Studies across the fields of literature, folklore, and rhetoric in the Department was broad and deep enough to merit strong praise from the April 2000 Visiting Review Team.[11] The review team's letter to chair James Phelan dedicates a paragraph to African American Literature:

The African American group has a number of strengths, which helps account for the Department's ability to have mounted once again a successful junior search. Whereas too many African Americanists in English departments

11. The review is dated April 13, 2000, and the reviewers were Michael Martone, Professor of English and Director of the Program in Creative Writing at The University of Alabama; Katherine O'Brien O'Keeffe, Professor of English, University of Notre Dame; Brook Thomas, Professor of English and Comparative Literature, The University of California, Irvine; and Kathleen E. Welch, Professor of English, University of Oklahoma.

have to work in relative isolation, the English Department at Ohio State has seven African Americanists, a depth allowing for collaborative work both within the Department and without. For instance, a second strength is the connection African American has with other areas in the Department, notably folklore and rhetoric and composition. Only one other department in the country comes close to having the overlapping strength between African American literature and rhetoric and composition that Ohio State has.

The reviewers go on to point out the close ties of the Department of English to the Department of African and African American Studies, and the potential to develop Asian American literature and an American Studies program. The paragraph continues by stating, "The department has already assembled one of the best, if not the best, group of African Americanists in the Big Ten, which is quite an accomplishment in itself," and the paragraph ends by stating that if senior hiring continues at this accelerated rate and strength (through selective investment hires), the Department could "become the best group in the country other than Harvard." What this report did not foresee was that Roberts, Royster, and Lee would all become senior administrators.

Nevertheless, under Lee's chairship during the years 2002–2009, African American Literature continued to flourish with the hiring of nine African Americanists of various ethnicities and subspecialties. A sampling of the titles of their selected scholarly works showcases the departmental expansion of the field during the new millennium: Adélékè Adéèkó (*The Slave's Rebellion: Literature, History, Orature*); Stephanie Brown (*The Postwar African-American Novel: Protest and Discontent, 1945–1950*); Cynthia Callahan (*Kin of Another Kind: Transracial Adoption in American Literature*); Ryan Freedman (*Hollywood's African American Films: The Transition to Sound*); Lynn Itagaki ("1992 Los Angeles Crisis and the Post-Civil Rights Era" [in progress]); Valerie Lee (*Granny Midwives & Black Women Writers: Double-Dutched Readings*); Koritha Mitchel (*Living with Lynching: African American Lynching Plays, Performance, and Citizenship, 1890–1930*); Martin Joseph Ponce (*Beyond the Nation: Diasporic Filipino Literature and Queer Reading*); John Roberts (*From Trickster to Badman: The Black Folk Hero in Slavery and Freedom*); and Andreá Williams (*Dividing Lines: Class Anxiety and Postbellum Black Fiction*). The breadth of expertise in African American Literature was enriched by the concurrent hirings of such colleagues as postcolonialist Pranav Jani, a courtesy appointment given to Valerie Kinloch (Education and Human Ecology), and by many colleagues already on the faculty who reenvisioned the way they taught their respective historical fields. Of course, African American Literature also was enriched by the larger area of African American Rhetoric:

Beverly Moss (*A Community Text Arises: A Literature Text and a Literacy Tradition in African-American Churches*) and Jacqueline Jones Royster (*Traces of a Stream: Literacy and Social Change among African American Women*).

During the late 1990s Department chair James Phelan and the Executive Committee crafted a document that prepared the way for the expansion of African American Literature. Supported by all of the Department's area groups, the memo[12] "clearly affirm[ed] the Department's commitment to a diversity of people and ideas." The document outlined five guiding principles for pursuing diversity in the Department:

1. We ought not to assume that there is a one-to-one correspondence between subject matter and individual identity (e.g., if one is African American, one must study some aspect of African American culture).

2. We ought, therefore, to welcome scholars who are members of underrepresented groups who are working on subjects traditionally dominated by members of the majority group. Similarly, scholars who are members of the majority group ought not to regard, say, ethnic literatures or minority discourse, as subject matters that are off-limits to them.

3. We ought not to assume that the responsibility for diversity rests largely with one area group (e.g., twentieth-century) or with those of us who are members of underrepresented groups. The responsibility needs to be shared by the whole Department.

4. We need to monitor our curriculum and to construct our syllabi so that diversity of texts and ideas is appropriately represented. Our training of graduate students as teachers and scholars should continue to address issues of diversity.

5. We need to attend to our local culture, particularly to the demographics of our student body, as we make particular decisions about such matters as faculty and graduate student recruitment. Attending to local culture also means attending to the climate for members of underrepresented groups in the Department, the College, and the University.

These guidelines for pursuing diversity have withstood the test of time as a valuable template for doing diversity in the academy.

---

12. Dated July 1, 1998 and addressed to the "English Department Faculty, Students, and Staff" from "Jim Phelan, for the 1997–98 Executive Committee," the memo was titled "Diversity Statement" and consisted of a preamble, general principles, guidelines for pursuing diversity, obstacles to achieving diversity, and ideas for increasing diversity.

In sum, the Department of English now offers a varied undergraduate and graduate slate of courses in US Ethnic and Postcolonial Literatures, most notably African American Literature:[13]

- 2281 Introduction to African-American Literature
- 2291 US Literature: 1865 to Present
- 4581 Special Topics in US Ethnic Literatures
- 4582 Special Topics in African-American Literature
- 4583 Special Topics in World Literature in English
- 4586 Studies in American Indian Literature and Culture
- 4587 Studies in Asian American Literature and Culture
- 4588 Studies in Latino/a Literature and Culture
- 6757.01 Introduction to Graduate Study in African-American Literature, 1746–1900
- 6757.02 Introduction to Graduate Study in African-American Literature, 1900 to Present
- 6758 Introduction to Graduate Study in US Ethnic Literature and Culture
- 6760 Introduction to Graduate Study in Postcolonial Literature and Theory
- 7851 Seminar in Critical Approaches to Black Literature
- 7858 Seminar in US Ethnic Literatures and Culture
- 7864 Postcolonial/Transnational Literatures

> they ask me to remember
> but they want me to remember
> their memories
> and I keep on remembering mine
> —Lucille Clifton

It is daunting to contribute history to a department with archival material labeled "The Estrich Years," "The Dasher Papers," and "The Thurber Album." As someone who entered the Department as a graduate student unaware of the greatness around her and as a colleague used to teaching texts that offer alternative histories, I take liberty to follow the advice of a twelve-fingered mother of six, African American poet Lucille Clifton. Clifton recommends that one remember her own memories. The history of the Department that I carry most intimately with me

---

13. This list of courses reflects offerings as of the 2015–16 academic year.

begins on a hot August day in 1973 when, clad in my favorite leather sandals, a pair of jeans, and a multicolored top, I walked into Denney Hall eager to register for my doctoral classes. Unbeknownst to me at the time, three years prior to my arrival, several of the professors in the Department of English had been active in the campus disorders of 1970. When I became chair of the Department, I stumbled upon documents that would flesh out my historical view of the era. One such document was "The O. S. U. Campus Disorders of 1970: A Personal View" by Emeritus Professor of English, Charles B. Wheeler.[14] From this document I learned that the Ohio State campus, as with 760 other campuses, was riddled and strapped by student unrest and that residents of Denney Hall had a ringside view of the happenings on the Oval and outside Bricker Hall. Wheeler describes a scene populated by the National Guard, civilian soldiers with loaded weapons, and professors tear-gassed as they were leaving Denney Hall. Two fires were set in Denney offices and elsewhere, and eventually the University had to close down. Wheeler explains that "the strike at OSU had been called originally because of what was felt to be the University's unresponsiveness to two sets of demands, the first by the Afro-Am Society and the second by an Ad Hoc group, so called, which swept together every other issue that could possibly be presented and merged them with the blacks' demands." Originally crafted on his old Royal typewriter, Wheeler's essay is a good read on campus politics, media interventions, race, class, popular culture, and the rhetoric of strikers and faculty members.

I walked into this post-riot climate aware that students nationwide were demanding a more open canon in fields such as literature. A product of several private institutions, I had not read much African American Literature, but Ellison's *Invisible Man* was enough to make me want to read/demand more. Here I was, a twenty-three-year-old strolling by the professors' offices when I noticed one man who looked to me to be a rather handsome "brother." Because I had never met a black person in my life with the last name of "Beja," I entertained the possibility that I could be wrong. Nonetheless, I remember telling my advisor to sign me up for whatever he was teaching. (To this day, I understand graduate students who sign up for classes for less than noble reasons). I would later learn from Murray Beja that what I mistook for "blackness" was actually Sephardic Jewish "swarthiness." But some of my instincts were correct. Early on during my graduate days, I stumbled on a journal article by Murray that argued for the importance

14. Wheeler wrote a five-page single-spaced on-the-spot account in 1970 and then in 1993 supplemented his account with more recent reflections. He writes, "So it was with a curious kind of binocular vision that I re-read it: vividly recalling through the mind's eye the look and feel of these events, once more in the midst, and at the same time standing outside of them with the perspective of more than two decades of intervening history, during which time I myself had changed along with the world I lived in."

of African American literature.[15] That essay gave me the courage to pursue African American Literature at a time when there were no actual courses in African American Literature.

There was, however, Patrick Mullen's folklore classes and independent studies. I remember calling home to tell my sister that all those folk rhymes, hand games, and toasts that she and I voiced while growing up, and the way Booty, and Big Man, and Ray-Ray played the dozens were all in a book called *Motherwit from the Laughing Barrel* by Alan Dundes. Who would have imagined that our experiences were fodder for academic scholarship? At the time I thought that folklore was a backdoor way of building a background in African American Literature, but I now see it as a foundational flooring as important to African American Literature as Greek mythology is to Western Literature at large.

Even as I was taking graduate courses, I was aware that there were two African American professors who taught undergraduate courses: Carl Marshall and Hortense Thornton. Decades later John Roberts would send me an email that helped me realize that although Marshall and Thornton taught only undergraduate courses, I would have benefitted from their mentorship:

> I can't forget Carl Marshall who, though not an African Americanist, knew the canon well. He also knew quite a bit about folklore. Although not one to do outreach to African American students, he was very welcoming if you sought him out. He was not only on my dissertation committee, but he also did independent studies with practically all of us. . . . He was actually the one who called my attention to Baldwin's fascination with African American music. One of my regrets is that I did not seek him out to thank him for all he did for me as a grad student before he passed.

> And while Thornton's tenure at OSU was short, she kind of paved the way for the acceptance of African American literature in the Department. Her classes were always packed. She allowed Trudier, Joe, and me to sit in on her undergraduate classes to get the sweep of African American literature. (We had no background to speak of coming to OSU.) In her own kind of wacky way, she served as the center of black community in the Department the first year that I was there and longer for Joe and Trudier. Her door was always open to us, and she made a point to make sure that we were okay.[16]

---

15. Morris Beja, "It Must Be Important: Negroes in Contemporary American Fiction," *Antioch Review 24* (Fall 1964): 323–336. As with Robert Bone's *Negro Novel in America* (1958; 2nd edition, 1965), Beja's essay was one of the earliest affirmations predicting the necessity of studying Black literature.

16. John Roberts, now Vice President of Isaacson, Miller search firm, shared this information with me in a personal email dated February 10, 2015.

This type of mentorship would have served me well when I was warned by one professor that I should not write a dissertation on African American Literature because it would be a waste of my brains, and the field would "blow over" before I finished writing the dissertation. I hedged my bets by writing a dissertation on Melville and Ellison, prompted by ideas gleaned from a two-quarter seminar on Melville taught by Julian Markels, and I formed a dissertation committee of Markels, Mullen, and O. R. Dathorne from African American and African Studies. At the dissertation defense we were joined by Frank W. Hale, Jr., Associate Dean of the Graduate School, for whom the Frank W. Hale, Jr. Black Cultural Center is named. My lack of confidence in focusing solely on African American literature was not in the literature itself, for by this time I had read Jean Toomer's *Cane*, most of Langston Hughes's poetry, Nella Larsen's *Passing*, and short stories by Alice Walker and Ernest Gaines, as well as a list of titles several pages long. Additionally, Toni Morrison had already published *The Bluest Eye* and *Sula*. My lack of confidence was not with the authors, but with an academy that might not be ready to hire an African American African Americanist.

There was no need to worry. After having spent fifteen years at my first employer, Denison University, where I did get to teach a wide range of multicultural literatures, I returned to teach at Ohio State. Hired in 1991 as an African Americanist, I was on a mission to graduate a second wave of African Americanists to carry on the type of work that Trudier Harris, John Roberts, Charles Rowell, and others performed. Mostly from small southern schools, this earlier cohort fought for acceptance in a Department not yet comfortable with the ambitions of African American students doing literary studies. In looking over discursive graduate reports—another set of documents I stumbled upon while Chair—I saw that the earlier generation of my colleagues wrote comments about race and the South that certainly must have dampened the spirits of students who would one day have stellar careers.[17] The third cohort of doctoral students (from the late 1990s–2015) consisted of a larger cohort of students coming to study African American Literature, Folklore, Culture, and Theory, with some coming from as far as Japan, Germany, and Greece. Among this latter cohort receiving their doctorates were: Tiffany Anderson (Youngstown State); Bennis Blue (Virginia State University); Chiaki Ishikawa (Rikkyo University); Corrie Claiborne (Morehouse College); Tayo Clyburn (Executor Director of Mission and Strategic Partnerships, Office of Diversity and Inclusion, Ohio State); Kalenda Eaton (University of Nebraska; Arcadia University); Rosemary Hathaway (University of West Virginia); Esther Jones (E. Franklin Frazier Chair of African American Literature,

---

17. Around 2013 the Department finally eliminated the practice of requiring professors to write graduate reports for each of their students. African American students had borne the brunt of such comments as "uneducable," "profoundly neurotic," and "wretched writing."

Theory and Culture, Clark University); Christopher Lewis (Western Kentucky University); Antonia MacDonald-Smythe (Associate Dean, St. George's University, Grenada); Brandon Manning (University of Nevada—Las Vegas); Eleni Mavromatidou (Ohio State Post-Doc Research Scholar); Aaron Oforlea (Washington State University); Candice Pipes (US Air Force Academy); and Eva Thompson (Kennesaw University).

When elected Chair of English in 2002, I could not help but remember my early years in the Department as a young graduate student seeking to do African American Literature. Coming from smaller Northeastern and Midwestern private institutions with fewer than fifty buildings, I relished strolling among the almost 500 buildings of Ohio State. My cigar-smoking male professors wore uncollared, unbuttoned shirts and were more liberal in spirit than what my provincial background was used to. They were closer to the English professors I saw on television and in the movies. They even taught some class sessions in their homes. Etched in my memory are the photos of children on the mantle of Ed Corbett's fireplace, as well as discussing Joyce's *Ulysses* for hours at Murray Beja's home.[18] And although I made it clear that I was interested mostly in African American Literature, I appreciated the fact that Tony Libby never batted an eye when I asked him to oversee my directed study in W. B. Yeats and Wallace Stevens.[19] It is the Department's elasticity, flexibility, and intellectual integrity that opened its doors to African American Literature. I am proud of the Department to which I owe my literary life.

18. I talk more about the professors because I remember only one student from my actual classes—a woman with long grayish/white hair who talked all the time in Corbett's History of Rhetoric class, a course I signed up for because Rhetoric was as elusive a term to me as folklore. This classmate was Andrea Lunsford—before she became Andrea Lunsford. At the time, and not knowing that I was sitting beside Corbett's *heir apparent,* I thought Andrea was faking the pleasure of what I considered rather boring material. I laugh now. Outstanding rhetorician that she is, Andrea's pleasure was for real.

19. I am always amazed by what nuggets of experiences students remember. In a February 10, 2016 email from Trudier Harris to me, she writes: "I have fond memories of Robert (Bob) Jones, who allowed me to stay at his home when I arrived for grad school because the dorms were not opened. We still exchange news at Christmas time. . . . Then, I met Beja in my first summer classes at OSU in 1969. I will always remember that he pointed me out in class as being the only person who answered correctly an identification question about a Yeats poem ('nose pressed to a sweet-shop window'). And, of course, Pat Mullen was wonderful during my entire time at OSU. Fran Utley was helpful and encouraging as well. Overall, my experience at OSU (after I got over trying to quit in my second quarter) turned out well, and I am grateful for the training that has enabled me to have a stellar career."

Still another extremely important appointment made in 1991 was that of Linda Mizejewski, the first faculty member hired as a "film" person, as well as in feminist theory. Linda, who was promoted in 1994 and again in 2000, received the University Alumni Award for Distinguished Teaching in 2004 and the Arts and Sciences Harlan Hatcher Distinguished Faculty Award in 2009. She is the author of *Divine Decadence: Fascism, Female Spectacle, and the Makings of Sally Bowles* (1992); *Ziegfeld Girl: Image and Icon in Culture and Cinema* (1999); *Hardboiled and High Heeled: The Woman Detective in Popular Culture* (2004); *It Happened One Night* (2010); and *Pretty/Funny: Women Comedians and Body Politics* (2014).

We're pleased that Linda, who left the Department of English in 2006 and is currently in the Department of Women's, Gender and Sexuality Studies, as well as the Department of Comparative Studies, the Diversity and Identity Studies Collective, and of course the Film Studies Program, has provided us with the following account of the role of film studies within the English Department.

FILM STUDIES IN THE ENGLISH DEPARTMENT

Linda Mizejewski

In the 1970s, English departments studied literature, but by the 1980s, new theoretical lenses made it possible to study "texts"—popular journalism, television, advertising, films—all fair game as topics for scholarship. Film studies in particular grew as a field because of exciting developments through psychoanalytic and semiotic theory. A number of scholars trained in literary studies began to extend their work into film. A good example is John Hellmann, whom the English Department had hired in 1977 to teach twentieth-century American literature at the Lima Campus. Hellmann broadened his research into historicist and cultural studies and began publishing film scholarship in 1982. His subsequent scholarship crosses several media, and he continues to teach film courses at Lima and to serve as an integral part of the OSU Film Studies Program.

In the 1980s, there was no such program, and though there were outstanding film scholars at OSU such as Judith Mayne and Ron Green, film studies was formally located in a Department of Photography and Cinema that did not survive administrative reorganization in 1990. At the main campus English Department, the active film scholar was Department Chair Murray Beja, whose 1979 book *Film and Literature* was among the first serious adaptation studies to treat film as film. Modernist scholar Tony Libby was also doing work in film studies. Beja introduced the Department's first film course, Film and Literature, which by 1990 was popular enough to be taught as a large-lecture course (100–120 students), and through the 1980s it was taught with a 16 mm projector.

I was hired in 1991 for a Film and Literature position, though it was clear that the Department was more interested in the former than the latter for me. They wanted someone formally trained in film studies to expand course offerings and help build that field in the Department. Between 1991 and 1999, I developed three new courses: an introductory undergraduate Film Analysis course, an upper-division Topics in Film course, and a graduate seminar, Introduction to Graduate Studies in Film. Beja and I also worked out a way to avoid a separate class meeting as a screening day for film courses; the quarter system was generous enough in its time slots that we could schedule one class meeting a week that was long enough to introduce and screen a film, followed by a second shorter follow-up class meeting—a schedule structure that remained in place until the less-flexible semester system was implemented in 2012.

The resources for film studies were, throughout the University, somewhat scarce in the early 1990s. The use of 16 mm projectors had just recently been discontinued, and the VHS projectors were not high quality. Beja complied with my request for a laser-disc player so I could show high-quality clips for my graduate course. The disc player sat on my office desk, and I would carry it over to Lord Hall and set it up in a basement room that even with heavy blinds could not be totally darkened. The University's film library was a little collection of VHS tapes also in the Lord Hall basement, guarded by a Christian staff member who frowned her disapproval over certain titles. When I taught a course on gay and queer cinema with Thomas Piontek, she refused to allow undergraduates to borrow titles like *Rock Hudson's Home Movies* and *No Skin off My Ass* until I lodged a formal complaint.

In 1999, the Department hired Jared Gardner for a position in American literature, though a good deal of his work was in film studies. He'd been advised not to mention film during his job interview, but when he dropped a reference to DeMille's *Cheat* in his job talk, several of us lit up. Half of Gardner's course assignments were in film studies, and he quickly became part of OSU's growing Film Studies Program. Gardner redesigned the introductory Film Analysis class into a large-lecture course, and he soon became a leader in Popular Culture Studies at OSU.

The first Ph.D. students to focus on film were Dennis Aig (1983)—and James Griffith (1984) and Dennis Bingham (1990), both of whom turned their dissertations into books. Matt Ramsey (2002) wrote a dissertation on adaptations of Faulkner and became a Faulkner/cultural studies scholar; another graduate, Todd McGowan (1996) became a well-known Lacanian film scholar, so though his dissertation was in literature, he started work on film in our graduate seminars.

The Department advertised for a film specialist in 2006 following my move to another department, and because the two top candidates were equally outstanding, Department Chair Valerie Lee convinced the dean to hire both of them. Sean O'Sullivan and Ryan Friedman were perfect fits with Departmental strengths: O'Sullivan in narrative theory and Friedman in cultural studies. Together with Gardner, they developed an advanced graduate course, Seminar in Film and Media.

Meanwhile, Film Studies at OSU had developed into an interdisciplinary program which by 2000 administered an undergraduate major and minor and a graduate specialization. In 2016, a Master's Degree in Film Studies was approved by the Board of Regents. The English Department's film courses were central to all of these curricula; its two graduate courses were core courses for the new M.A., and its three undergraduate courses were part of the Film Studies major and minor. In 2015, Ryan Friedman became OSU's Director of Film Studies, capping the English Department's long history of leadership in the field.

There were other important hires in 1991 as well, in the field of American literature, including Elizabeth Renker, who went on to be promoted in 1997 and 2008. Her *Strike through the Mask: Herman Melville and the Scene of Writing* appeared in 1996. We have earlier in this history had cause to cite her valuable study *The Origins of American Literature Studies: An Institutional History* (2007). She is also the editor of *Poems: A Concise Anthology* (2015). Elizabeth received a Fellowship from the American Council of Learned Societies in 2018. She has received the University Alumni Award for Distinguished Teaching (2008) and other teaching awards as well: the Rodica C. Botoman Award for Distinguished Undergraduate Teaching and Mentoring (2006); the English Department's Graduate Professor of the Year Award (2010) and its Undergraduate Professor of the Year Award (2012); and Sigma Tau Delta's Honorary Professor of the Year recognition (2012). In 2014, she was one of the inaugural recipients of the Ronald and Deborah Ratner Distinguished Teaching Award in the College of Arts and Sciences, Division of Arts and Humanities (2014).

Also hired in American literature in 1991 was Susan S. Williams; she was promoted in 1997 and 2006. Susan is the author of *Confounding Images: Photography and Portraiture in Antebellum American Fiction* (1997) and *Reclaiming Authorship: Literary Women in America, 1850–1900* (2006). She has co-edited, with Steven Fink, *Reciprocal Influences: Literary Production, Distribution, and Consumption in America* (1999) and has edited an edition of Hawthorne's *Scarlet Letter* (2006). She has received both the University Alumni Award for Distinguished Teaching (2005) and the Distinguished Faculty Service Award

(2007), as well as the Founder's Award of the Academy of Teaching (2015), for promoting teaching excellence at the University. She has served as Vice Provost in the Office of Academic Affairs and is currently Vice Dean in the College of Arts and Sciences.

The year 1992 marked the 500th anniversary of the voyage of Christopher Columbus—the Columbian Quincentenary. As early as 1988, as a project begun with the Center for Medieval and Renaissance Studies, members of the Department—notably CMRS Director Christian Zacher, David Frantz, and David Citino—began to organize an array of academic contributions to the commemoration, as a significant element of the celebration highlighting the name of OSU's city. Zacher oversaw this planning, raised money—some of it from the Office of Academic Affairs—for events, and with the help of colleagues in and outside the Department, devised a series of cultural events, conferences, scholarly meetings, and exhibitions on Columbus and his era. He obtained NEH funding for the exchange of OSU faculty with the University of Genoa, and, in partnership with Frantz and colleagues in French and Italian, translated the major Italian documents of Columbus's life. Events included various exhibits originating in Italy. Department faculty also supplied historical support for the city's most popular productions for the Quincentenary, the replica of Columbus's ship the Santa Maria, and Ameriflora, an international horticultural exposition located in Franklin Park.

Arnie Shapiro retired in 1992. Steve Fink took over as Vice Chair, and Jim Phelan took on Arnie's duties as chair of the New Personnel Committee—with no fewer than eight faculty appointments authorized that year.

In Creative Writing, the Department was joined by Lore Segal as a full Professor. Lore, a frequent contributor to the *New Yorker,* is the author of such novels as *Other People's Houses* (1964), *Lucinella* (1976), and *Her First American* (1985), and of children's literature, for example *The Story of Mrs. Lovewright and Purrless Her Cat* (1985), and, with Maurice Sendak, an edition of *The Juniper Tree and Other Tales from Grimm* (1973), which she also translated. Lore retired in 1997.

Jacqueline Jones Royster, who had been a visiting faculty member Winter Quarter of 1991 while at Spelman College, came back to the Department as an Associate Professor, also in 1992, with interests in the rhetorical history of African American women, literacy, and the teaching of writing. She is the author of *Double Stitch: Black Women Write about Mothers and Daughters* (1991); *Traces of a Stream: Literacy and Social Change among African American Women* (2000); and *Profiles of Ohio Women, 1803–2003* (2003); and the editor of *Southern Horrors and Other Writings: The Anti-Lynching Campaign of*

FIGURE 8.11. Susan S. Williams

THE OHIO STATE UNIVERSITY COMMEMORATES COLUMBUS

FIGURE 8.12. The Columbus Quincentenary

Ida B. Wells, 1892–1900 (1997) and the co-editor of *Calling Cards: Theory and Practice in the Study of Race, Gender, and Culture* (2005). Jacqueline went on to act as Senior Vice Provost and Executive Dean of the Colleges of the Arts and Sciences and left OSU in 2010 to become Dean of the Ivan Allen College of Liberal Arts at Georgia Tech. She had received the ADE Francis Andrew March Award from the MLA, which recognizes distinguished service to the profession of English, in 2006.

Brenda Jo Brueggemann came to the Department as a specialist in rhetoric and disability studies; she was promoted in 1999 and 2008. Brenda is the author of *Lend Me Your Ear: Rhetorical Constructions of Deafness* (1999) and *Deaf Subjects between Identities and Places* (2009). She is the co-editor of the MLA volume *Disability Studies: Enabling the Humanities* (2002); *Literacy and Deaf People: Cultural and Contextual Perspectives* (2004); *Women and Deafness: Double Visions* (2006); and, with Wendy Hesford, of *Rhetorical Visions: Reading and Writing in a Visual Culture* (2007). Brenda left OSU for her alma mater, the University of Louisville, in 2013. She is currently the Professor and Aetna Chair of Writing at the University of Connecticut.

Keeping with 1992: Luke Wilson was appointed in Renaissance literature, with a focus on legal history. He is the author of *Theaters of Intention: Drama and the Law in Early Modern England* (2000). He was promoted in 1998. Luke is married to colleague Sandra Macpherson.

Also that year the Department hired Karen Winstead in medieval literature. Karen is the author of *Virgin Martyrs: Legends of Sainthood in Late Medieval England* (1997) and *John Capgrave's Fifteenth Century* (2007) and of several editions and translations of medieval saints' lives. She was promoted in 1998 and 2007. She received the English Undergraduate Organization's Professor of the Year award in 2016.

Scott De Witt was hired at the Marion campus that year; promoted to Associate Professor in 1998, he was brought to the Columbus campus in 2002 to direct the Digital Media Project, the Department's digital media production and teaching studio. He is the author of *Writing Inventions: Identities, Technologies, Pedagogies* (2002), which was awarded the "Computers and Composition Distinguished Book Award" in 2003. With H. Lewis Ulman and Cynthia Selfe he edited *Stories That Speak to Us: Exhibits from the Digital Archive of Literacy Narratives* (2013). Scott received the University Alumni Award for Distinguished Teaching in 1999.

In 1992 the University also gained *Narrative*, when what was then the Society for the Study of Narrative Literature changed the title of the *Journal of Narrative Literature*; *Narrative* became a publication of The Ohio State University Press, with James Phelan as its editor. Its first issue came out in January 1993.

Figure 8.13 barely hints at one significant change in the makeup of the Department over the decade. In 1983–84, there were eleven women faculty at the tenured or tenure-track level in the English Department (none of them a full Professor); in 1993–94, there were forty-four tenured or tenure-track women (including five full Professors). The changes went on to be even more dramatic, of course.[20]

Morris Beja left the position of Chair at the end of the 1993–94 year, after eleven years, as James Phelan took over as Interim Chair. Murray has continued his scholarship, in both Joyce and film studies. He has published two volumes of Joyce criticism, one edited with his wife, Ellen Carol Jones, with whom he has also co-edited a collection of essays on film, *Cinematic Narratives: Transatlantic Perspectives* (2018). He published a memoir of his childhood and youth in the Bronx, *Tell us about . . .: A Memoir*, in 2011. Since his retirement in 2001 he has had visiting professorships at Northwestern University and Beijing Foreign Studies University.

One project that he has greatly enjoyed is working, with Chris Zacher, on this history of the Department of English.

---

20. As of this writing, there are in the Department thirty tenured or tenure-track women faculty—ten of them full Professors.

FIGURE 8.13. Faculty of the Department of English, 1994

Fourth row: Sebastian Knowles, Roger Cherry, John King, David Riede, Georgina Kleege, Nicholas Howe, Richard Martin, Jon Erickson, Thomas Piontek, Grantland Rice, Luke Wilson, Rick Livingston, Anthony Libby. *Third row:* Steven Fink, Susan Williams, Clare Simmons, Karen Winstead, Ruth Lindenborg, James Battersby, Marlene Longenecker, Lisa Kiser, Kathy Fagan, Michelle Herman, Amy Shuman, Mary Pat Martin, Valerie Lee. *Second row:* Kitty Locker, Mark Conroy, Frank Donoghue, Jeredith Merrin, James Phelan, Christopher Highley, Elizabeth Renker. *First row:* Kay Halasek, Frank O'Hare, Morris Beja, Sara Garnes, Alan Brown.

CHAPTER 9

From the Omnibus to the Federation

The Phelan Years

BY JAMES PHELAN

THOUGHT EXPERIMENT: imagine sliding into the driver's seat of a speeding and seemingly ever-expanding (omni)bus, just as the previous driver, who has been going like gangbusters for eleven years, slides out.

You now have a sense of how I felt in the Spring of 1994 when David Frantz, then Acting Dean of the College of Humanities, persuaded me to become Interim Chair. I was simultaneously scared and exhilarated, worried that I'd be the new poster boy for the Peter Principle and buoyed by David's confidence in me. I coped in part by reflecting on my previous seventeen years of experience in the Department, which had taught me that the bus was sturdy, that Murray Beja had it heading toward great things, and that I could count on getting lots of advice from my fellow passengers. By Autumn 1994, I told those passengers I was willing to keep driving, and, perhaps for lack of an alternative, they said they were willing to let me.

Eight years later, we had substantial success to celebrate. Among the highlights, English won the University's Departmental Teaching Award (offered only for a few years in the 1990s) and an Eminent Scholar position in rhetoric and composition (given to the Department in 2002 and filled in 2004 with the hiring of Harvey Graff). In addition, the Department had been chosen as one of only eleven in the University to receive Selective Investment (SI) funding and had begun using that funding for senior hiring in medieval studies (Richard Green and Alastair Minnis), the Renaissance (Richard Dutton), Twentieth-Century American literature and culture (Brian McHale), and creative writing (Andrew Hudgins and Erin McGraw). These achievements, which I'll discuss in more detail below, came in conjunction with developments both in the central administration of the University and in the Department that began to shift the overall configuration of the Department. The central administration sought to raise the scholarly profile of the University so that it would become known as a great public institution. Within the Department, different segments of the omnibus continued to grow and develop, which meant that they were inevitably more self-contained and inner-directed. Indeed, over time Murray's metaphor of the omnibus faded, and though no single alternative emerged, I suggest that a metaphor once suggested to me by Jared Gardner aptly captures the next phase of the Department's evolution: from 1994 until the present, the Department has evolved into a federation of (mostly) peacefully coexisting subfields.

Here's one way to characterize the difference between riding the omnibus and living in the federation. When I joined the Department as an Assistant Professor in 1977, I thought of myself as a member of the OSU English Department first and a critical theorist with interests in the novel second. I felt very fortunate to have been invited to board the Department's vehicle, where so many were already gathered, and to have the opportunity to contribute to our collective efforts in whatever ways Julian Markels and my other senior colleagues deemed appropriate. Today, I think of myself first as a core faculty member of both Project Narrative and an interdisciplinary group in the medical humanities. As a "Chair in recovery," I still regard being a member of the English Department as an important part of my scholarly identity, and I participate actively when we act collectively. But the proportion of my time spent on those collective efforts is significantly less than it used to be. Some things that we used to do either centrally, such as graduate admissions and course assignments, are now primarily done by subfields. Other things that still involve the collective, such as hiring and Promotion and Tenure, have given more weight to the subfields. In addition, there are more subfields than there were in 1977 (both of the subfields I've identified myself with here were not even glimmers in Julian's eye back then), and they are more active. I find that both the omnibus and the federation models are viable ways of organizing a large Department, and, as that great OSU philosopher Woody Hayes once said in a book title, "you win with people." But I'm also struck that while Murray Beja was explicitly attentive to the Department as omnibus, I did not set out to reconfigure it as a federation. Instead, I think the federation was the next logical evolutionary step, given our omnibus past and the University's vision of the future. I just happened to be Chair during the transition from one stage to the next.

In fact, when I began my term, one of the phrases I uttered most frequently was "intellectual community." It was my way of recharacterizing the omnibus, and my goal was to promote more interaction among the subfields. To that end, the Executive Committee in my first year helped establish once-a-quarter sessions devoted to faculty presenting work-in-progress. The Committee also helped start, under the banner of "Chat and Chow," a weekly, informal lunch at the Wexner Center for any faculty member who wanted to attend. The Executive Committee, as committee on committees, also recommended that we have a Social Committee and a December party-cum-talent-show before Christmas. All of these efforts were initially very successful: the first work-in-progress session was more like a one-day conference as multiple groups presented, and attendance was excellent. "Chat and Chow" brought together people who typically didn't have lunch together. The 1994 talent show was impressive for its range of performances from singing to storytelling, and it even featured a visit from St. Nicholas (the Department Chair in a Santa Claus suit borrowed from Linda Mizejewski). But over time these activities gradually lost their oomph, though the December party continued on in one form or another into Valerie Lee's term and has been revived by current chair Robyn Warhol. This progression, I think, was not because they were bad ideas badly executed but because the forces pulling us toward the federation were stronger than those pulling us toward "one large intellectual community."

Among those forces within the Department were two changes in how we did things that inevitably made subfields more prominent: hiring and annual reviews. During Julian's and Murray's terms, we did all our hiring in a given year through a single large committee of people from different fields, followed by collective decisions after campus visits. But sometimes those committee members felt insufficiently qualified to make the necessary qualitative discriminations between highly qualified candidates. So we moved to a model in which we had separate smaller committees for each position, ideally with two members of the committee from the hiring field and a third from a somewhat related field. The Chair (and after we split the job of Vice-Chair and Director of Undergraduate Studies into two, the Vice-Chair) would oversee the whole operation. We would still make collective decisions after campus visits, but everyone—including prospective hires and thus our new faculty—was being socialized to think "subfield first."

Based on input from assistant professors, we made some revisions to the annual review process so that they would receive more substantial feedback leading up to fourth-year and sixth-year reviews. In particular, we asked the assistant professors to submit samples of "work-in-progress," and we added a senior faculty member in the field to the review committee. This procedure has, I believe, worked well over the years. But note that it, too, sends a message about the importance of the subfield.

Turning to forces moving us toward a federation at the University level, I highlight the Selective Investment competition, which asked us to identify our strongest subfields. Indeed, I now think that at least some of the controversy in the Department about our participation in that competition stemmed from tensions associated with moving from the omnibus to the federation. As I explain what I mean, I will also shift from the previous pattern of discussing hiring by year to discussing it by subfield.

SELECTIVE INVESTMENT

The central administration's efforts to raise OSU's scholarly profile translated into an obsession with the University's place in the national rankings. It's bad enough that the football team loses to Michigan almost every year (this was the John Cooper era when Michigan won 10 out 13 games), but why should we be so far behind the School Up North in the rankings? Why can't our reputation be like that of a Virginia or a UCLA? Central administrators constructed a list of ten "aspirational peers" (mostly from the Big Ten and the Pac 10) against whom we should measure ourselves in everything from enrollments to faculty salaries. Selective Investment emerged as the centerpiece of the plan to achieve OSU's aspirations. The program, conceived by Provost Richard John Sisson and supported by Presidents E. Gordon Gee and his successor William Kirwan, focused on choosing key departments to receive substantial funding for the hiring of outstanding senior faculty. Investing in already strong departments, Sisson believed, could make them eminent. Achieving eminence in a dozen core departments would greatly enhance the reputation of the University as a whole. Move over, Wolverines, Bruins, and Cavaliers; here come the Buckeyes.

Provost Sisson's plan did not depend on an influx of new money from the state of Ohio, from donors, or from any other external source. Instead, he funded Selective Investment by imposing a 1% tax on the annual budgets of each College for a period of three years. Sisson then redistributed that money to the selected departments. More specifically, a chosen Department would receive $500K from the funds generated by the tax and $250K from its College. In addition, the Department would commit another $250K from its own regular hiring funds (i.e., funds made available by retirements and departures).

Sisson implemented the plan with annual competitions during the academic years 1997–98, 1998–99, and 1999–2000. Kermit Hall, the Dean of the College of Humanities from 1994 until 1999, made success in Selective Investment a high priority for his administration, and he nominated History and English as the contenders from the College. Dean Hall's successor in 1999, Michael Hogan, former chair of History, placed a similar emphasis on success.

In 1997–98, the competition was primarily among the deans, who made pitches on behalf of their chosen departments, but neither History nor English was selected. In 1998–99, the University began trumpeting Selective Investment more loudly, and the competition became more open and required more from the contending departments: detailed proposals about why they were deserving and how they would use the hiring funds, and, then, if they made an initial cut, formal presentations before the Provost's committee that would choose the winners. These requirements meant that Selective Investment had to play out at the Department level. In English, we had to specify which of our many subfields would be awarded the new faculty positions and to provide a rationale for each choice, based on an assessment of the standing of the subfield in the Department and in the larger profession. We chose medieval, Renaissance, American, African American, creative writing, and rhetoric and composition.

When I circulated the proposal in 1998, many members of the Department expressed strong reservations about our entering the competition, and some expressed their outright opposition. These colleagues worried about what I think of as "intra-departmental selective investment," or, to put it another way, the loss of the single omnibus Department and the move to a federation in which some units would be more favored than others. Would SI mean that we would construct a de facto class division in the Department, with the SI subfields being the upper class and all the others the lower class? And would successful SI hiring only exacerbate such divisions? Those in favor of competing, including me, countered that SI hiring need not have these effects: the Department remained committed to all its subfields, and faculty in non-SI subfields would be valued—and evaluated—as they always had. In other words, the larger values of the federation would prevail.

If we hired well, we would add valuable colleagues who would contribute to the Department in multiple ways, not to mention that we'd increase the budget for faculty salaries in an unprecedented fashion. Furthermore, success in the competition would significantly raise the profile and status of the Department in the University, an outcome that would have ripple effects on future bids for resources from the College and the Office of Academic Affairs. More generally, through Selective Investment the University had decided to tie its own future reputation to the success of the winning Departments, a decision that meant the central administration would be deeply invested in their success. In short, we should compete because success would have major positive consequences—and we could be vigilant about avoiding the potential negative consequences.

In 1998–99, we went through the year-long competition—a process that included the Department's first official PowerPoint presentation to the Provost's committee—and made it to the finals. We were not chosen, but History was (I will not speculate on whether that choice was in any way related to Dean Hall's being a member of the History Department). We tried again in 1999–2000, the last year of the program, and we succeeded. English thus became one of thirteen Departments or programs in which the University had chosen to invest. In addition to History, the others were Chemistry, Mathematics, and Physics; Economics, Political Science, and Psychology; Neuroscience; Materials Science and Engineering and Electrical Engineering; the interdisciplinary program in cardiovascular bioengineering; and the College of Law.

Then came the hard but exciting work of doing the hiring, which was carried out over the next several years. In my last two years as Chair, we launched the searches in medieval, creative writing, Renaissance, and American, and, thanks to the work of many colleagues, especially the hiring committee chairs—Lisa Kiser for medieval, Michelle Herman for creative writing, John King for Renaissance, and Tony Libby for American—we had remarkable success. In the medieval search, we identified two outstanding candidates, Alastair Minnis and Richard Firth Green, and got permission from Dean Hogan to make offers to both. And both accepted—though we lost Alastair to Yale within a couple of years. In the creative writing search, we got appropriately creative with our hiring of Andrew Hudgins and Erin McGraw: we split the funds for the SI position and hired each on a 75% appointment. In the Renaissance search, we recruited Richard Dutton. In the American search, we hired Brian McHale. Valerie Lee became Chair in 2002, and during her first term she oversaw the completion of the SI hiring. With Kitty Locker and then Nan Johnson serving as committee chairs for the rhetoric and composition search, we hired Cynthia Selfe, and with Elizabeth Renker serving as committee chair for the African American position, we hired Adéléké Adéekó.

Although national rankings have the inertia of glaciers and SI did not have the effect on them that Provost Sisson had hoped, it proved to be a great boon to English. All of our hires made substantial contributions in teaching, research, and service, and collectively raised the profile of English within the University. Furthermore, the positive effects of having been selected lasted for many years. Rather than being restricted to SI hires, English received permission to hire in multiple non-SI fields. Although such matters are hard to calculate, I believe that our status as an SI Department—as well as our strength in Rhetoric and Composition—helped with our applications for the Ohio Eminent Scholar position that allowed us to hire Harvey Graff and for the Targeted Investment in Opportunity proposal that funded Project Narrative. As I write this piece, the identity of English as an SI Department has faded, but I am glad that this history provides an opportunity to remember how much the Department benefited from the program. As I write, Erin McGraw, Andrew Hudgins, Richard Green, Richard Dutton, and Cindy Selfe have all recently retired, so I am glad to have this opportunity on behalf of the whole Department to thank them—and Brian and Lékè as well—for their countless contributions to making the Department a better place.

MEDIEVAL

Richard Firth Green brought expertise in folklore, in medieval law and literature, and in drama as performance, and he was an exemplary citizen of the Department and the University. He served as Director of the Center for Medieval and Renaissance Studies from 2006 to 2013, and in the Presidency of the New Chaucer Society (2008–10). In addition to numerous articles in such journals as *Speculum, Medium Aevum, Chaucer Review,* and *Studies in the Age of Chaucer,* Richard is the author of *Elf Queens and Holy Friars: Fairy Beliefs and the Medieval Church* (2016), *A Crisis of Truth: Literature and Law in Ricardian England* (1998), and *Poets and Princepleasers: Literature and the English Court in the Late Middle Ages* (1980).

Richard's hiring helped round out our collection of strong scholars in the earliest periods of English literature and culture. In 1995 we hired Ethan Knapp as an assistant professor specializing in the later part of the period. An award-winning teacher, Ethan is the author of *The Bureaucratic Muse: Thomas Hoccleve and the Literature of Late Medieval England* (2001) and co-editor of *The Art of Vision: Ekphrasis in Medieval Literature and Culture* (2015). Ethan edits the Ohio State University Press book series, Interventions: New Studies in Medieval Literature.

In 2000 we hired Christopher Andrew (Drew) Jones as a specialist in the Anglo-Saxon period. Although he briefly left OSU for Notre Dame (2004–05), we were delighted to hire him back in 2005. Drew was delighted in turn because it meant he could be with his partner, Leslie Lockett, another Anglo-Saxonist, whom we had hired after she received her Ph.D. from Notre Dame in 2004. A stalwart citizen of the Department, Drew is the co-author of *The Relatio metrica de duobus ducibus: A Twelfth-Century Cluniac Poem on Prayer for the Dead* (2016); *Old English Shorter Poems, Volume I: Religious and Didactic* (2012); *A Lost Work by Amalarius of Metz: Interpolations in Salisbury, Cathedral Library, MS. 154.* (2001); and *Ælfric's Letter to the Monks of Eynsham* (1998).

CREATIVE WRITING

By hiring Andrew Hudgins and Erin McGraw in 2001, we added an award-winning poet and an accomplished fiction writer to our already thriving creative writing program. Andrew's books include *A Clown at Midnight* (2013); *American Rendering: New and Selected Poems* (2010); *Shut Up, You're Fine: Poems for Very, Very Bad Children* (2009); *Ecstatic in the Poison* (2003); *Babylon in a Jar* (2001); *The Glass Anvil* (1997); *The Glass Hammer: A Southern Childhood* (1994); *After the Lost War: A Narrative* (1988); *The Never-Ending* (1991); and *Saints and Strangers* (1985). Andrew also did a book of creative nonfiction, *The Joker: A Memoir* (2013). He was a finalist for the Pulitzer Prize in poetry for *Saints and Strangers* and a finalist for the National Book Award for *After the Lost War*. He has received the Ohioana Award for lifetime contributions to poetry in the state, and in 2007, he was inducted into the Fellowship of Southern Writers. Andrew retired in 2016.

We hired Erin McGraw at the rank of Associate Professor on the strength of her first two story collections, *Bodies at Sea* (1989) and *Lies of the Saints* (1996). We promoted her to Professor after the publication of *The Baby Tree* (2002), and Erin went on to write two more novels, *The Seamstress of Hollywood Boulevard* (2009), and *Better Food for a Better World* (2013), and another collection of stories, *The Good Life* (2014). Erin is a recipient of the University's Alumni Distinguished Teaching Award (2013). Erin retired in 2015.

The hiring of Andrew and Erin marked the fifth and sixth appointments in creative writing that we made between 1995 and 2001, though, alas, three of those hires, fiction and creative nonfiction writer Bill Roorbach (1995–2001), fiction writer Melanie Rae Thon (1996–2000), and nonfiction writer Steven Kuusisto (2000–07) all moved on to other institutions for personal reasons. The remaining appointment was of Lee Martin, who joined us in 2001, and is now a College of Arts and Sciences Distinguished Professor.

FIGURE 9.1. Lee Martin

Lee is the author of the novels, *The Bright Forever* (2006, and a finalist for that year's Pulitzer Prize in Fiction); *Late One Night* (2016); *Break the Skin* (2011); *River of Heaven* (2009); and *Quakertown* (2001). He has also published three memoirs, *From Our House* (2000), *Turning Bones* (2003), and *Such a Life* (2012) as well as the writer's guide, *Telling Stories: The Craft of Narrative and the Writing Life* (2017). His first book was the short story collection, *The Least You Need to Know* (1996). Lee has served as Director of Creative Writing and has received the Alumni Award for Distinguished Teaching (2006).

RENAISSANCE

In this subfield, we made two hires of note: the first is our SI hire, Richard Dutton, whom we recruited in 2001–02 and who joined the Department in 2003. Richard not only delivered as a major scholar but he also distinguished himself as a Department citizen, taking leadership roles first as Vice-Chair for part of Valerie Lee's term and then succeeding her in the Chair's office from 2009 until 2013. Richard also served as Interim Chair in Spring 2014. Richard's scholarship includes *Ben Jonson: To the First Folio* (1983); *An Introduction to Literary Criticism* (1984); *Modern Tragicomedy and the British Tradition* (1986); *Mastering the Revels* (1991); *Ben Jonson: Authority: Criticism* (1996); *Licensing, Censorship, and Authorship in Early Modern England* (2000); *Ben Jonson, Volpone, and the Gunpowder Plot* (2008); and *Shakespeare: Court Dramatist* (2016). Richard retired in 2015.

The second notable hire was on the Mansfield campus, where Hannibal Hamlin began working as an assistant professor in 2000. Hannibal earned promotion and tenure to Associate Professor in 2005, and then transferred from Mansfield to Columbus in 2007 in part because we had a pressing need for someone to teach the course in the Bible as Literature. Hannibal is the author of *Psalm Culture and Early Modern English Literature* (2004) and *The Bible in Shakespeare* (2013). He is the editor of *The Sidney Psalter: The Psalms of Philip and Mary Sidney* (2009) and co-editor with Norman Jones of *The King James Bible after Four Hundred Years: Literary, Linguistic, and Cultural Influences* (2010).

AMERICAN

The first issue with the SI position was whether to hire in American to 1900 or in Twentieth-Twenty-First Centuries. Having recently hired two faculty in American to 1900, Jared Gardner and Elizabeth Hewitt (see below), we decided to go with the modernist/postmodernist period. We succeeded in recruiting Brian McHale, who joined the Department in 2002. Brian brought expertise not only in American literature, especially of the postmodernist period, but also in poetry and in narrative theory. When Brian and I (the Department's other narrative theorist in 2002) were joined by David Herman in 2004 and Frederick Aldama in 2005, we were well-positioned to compete for funding in the University's next competition, Targeted Investment in Excellence. Our success in that competition launched Project Narrative, whose story I tell later in this chapter. Brian is the author of *Postmodernist Fiction* (1987), *Constructing Postmodernism* (1992), *The Obligation toward the Difficult Whole* (2004), and *The Cambridge Introduction to Postmodernism* (2015). Brian has also done substantial editorial work, as Associate Editor and now Editor-in-Chief of *Poetics Today*, and as editor or co-editor of the following volumes: *The Edinburgh Companion to Twentieth-Century Literatures in English* (2006); *Teaching Narrative Theory* (2010); *The Cambridge Companion to Thomas Pynchon* (2012); *The Routledge Companion to Experimental Literature* (2012); and *The Cambridge History of Postmodern Literature* (2016). Brian received the University's Distinguished Scholar Award in 2016.

FIGURE 9.2. Brian McHale

In 1999, we had the opportunity to fill both a senior and a junior position in American to 1900, but two funny things happened on the way to those goals. We weren't happy with the senior candidates, and the junior candidate who emerged as our first choice, Jared Gardner, turned us down because we weren't able to offer a position to his spouse, Beth Hewitt—and because their home institution, Grinnell College, had taken various significant steps to retain both of them. Although we had other strong candidates for the junior position, we tried to think creatively: what if we asked Beth to apply for that position, and thought of Jared, who had already published his important book *Master Plots: Race and the Founding of an American Literature, 1787–1845* (1998), as the (young) senior hire? Late one night, I emailed Jared to inquire whether he and Beth would be open to this possibility, he promptly applied in the affirmative, and the rest is history.

In addition to continuing his work in American literature, Jared became an important contributor to Film Studies, was instrumental in establishing Popular Culture Studies, especially through his work on both film and comics, and has become a member of the core faculty of Project Narrative. In addition to *Master Plots*, Jared is the author of *The Rise and Fall of Early American Mag-*

azine Culture (2012) and *Projections: Comics and the History of Twenty-First Century Storytelling* (2012). He served as co-editor of the journal *American Periodicals* (2003–10) and is now editing *Inks: The Journal of the Comics Studies Society* and co-editing the OSU Press book series, Comics and Cartoons.

Beth's work too has expanded beyond the boundaries of American literature to 1900, especially in our curriculum where she now regularly teaches Science Fiction. She is the author of *Correspondence and American Literature, 1770–1865* (2005) and co-editor of both *The Letters and Early Epistolary Writings of Charles Brockden Brown* (2013) and *The American Register and Other Writings, 1807–1810*, volume 6 of the *Collected Writings of Charles Brockden Brown* (forthcoming). Beth and Jared have co-edited *Edgar Allan Poe: A Case Study in Critical Controversy* (2015).

RHETORIC, COMPOSITION, AND LITERACY

Although we did not do the SI hiring in rhetoric and composition until Valerie Lee's term, we made some valuable appointments in the field and added an important new unit, the Center for the Study and Teaching of Writing. CSTW, which subsumed the long-established tutorial functions of the Writing Center under the larger mission described in its title, was the brainchild of Andrea Lunsford, who was its first Director. Andrea used the leverage provided by a very attractive outside offer to help convince Dean Hall of the value of the Center. Although Andrea and Dean Hall both liked the idea of having the Center be independent of the Department—the Director of the Center reports not to the Chair of English but to the Dean—its main personnel has always come from the Department.

Andrea's eminence meant that she was frequently courted by other institutions, but it was not until Stanford came calling in 2001 that I ever felt we were in serious danger of losing her. It's easy to understand why Andrea would be attracted to an institution with Stanford's resources and reputation, especially since Stanford gave her a mandate to build a writing program there, making it one of the few premier private universities in the country to have such a program.

The loss of Andrea in 2001 was partially offset by other hiring that we did in rhetoric and composition during those years. In 1998, we hired James Fredal for a position in classical rhetoric, and in 2001 we hired Wendy Hesford for a position in rhetoric and writing studies. In addition, in 2002, we worked out the transfer of Scott DeWitt from the Marion campus to Columbus.

Jim Fredal is in the tradition of faculty such as Andrea, Valerie Lee, and John Roberts who are graduates of our own Ph.D. program, although he moved from graduate student to faculty member without first being employed at another university. Jim is the author of *Rhetorical Action in Ancient Athens: Persuasive Performance from Solon to Demosthenes* (2006) as well as award-winning essays on the Sophists and the enthymeme.

Wendy Hesford is the author of two award-winning books, *Framing Identities: Autobiography and the Politics of Pedagogy* (1999) and *Spectacular Rhetorics: Human Rights Visions, Recognitions, Feminisms* (2011), and co-editor with Wendy Kozol of two collections: *Haunting Violations: Feminist Criticism and the Crisis of the "Real"* (2001) and *Just Advocacy? Women's Human Rights, Transnational Feminisms, and the Politics of Representation* (2005). With Brenda Brueggemann, Wendy is the co-author of the textbook *Rhetorical Visions: Reading and Writing in a Visual Culture.*

We hired Scott DeWitt at the Marion campus in 1992, where he established himself as an outstanding contributor. In 1999 he received the Alumni Distinguished Teaching Award. His *Writing Inventions: Identities, Pedagogies, Technologies* (2001) won the Computer and Composition Distinguished Book Award in 2002. He did innovative things with the writing program at Marion. Meanwhile, in Columbus we had been expanding the scope of the Computers and Composition program, under the direction of Louie Ulman, John Norman, and Tony Libby. Indeed, the program had morphed into the Digital Media Project. But with Tony's retirement, John's not getting tenure, and Louie's move to become Associate Dean, we needed a new director. Although we did a national search, we eventually concluded that the best person for the job was our colleague in Marion. Scott was being recruited by other institutions, but we were able to persuade him to transfer to Columbus. Since the transfer, Scott has been director of the DMP as well as the First-Year Writing Program, and he has served as Vice-Chair for Rhetoric and Composition. Since 2005 Scott has directed or co-directed with Cindy Selfe, DMAC, the workshop on "Digital Media and Composition" that has instructed hundreds of teachers on incorporating digital media into their classrooms. Among other publications since moving to Columbus, Scott has co-edited with Louie Ulman and Cindy Selfe the digital collection *Stories That Speak to Us: Exhibits from the Digital Archive of Literacy Narratives* (2013).

BEYOND SI

Between 1994 and 2002 the Department was able to make significant appointments in other fields, particularly Folklore, Eighteenth-Century, Victorian, and Linguistics.

FOLKLORE

Dorothy (Dorry) Noyes joined the Department in 1996. She now has a joint appointment in Comparative Studies and courtesy appointments in Anthropology, French and Italian, and Germanic Languages and Literatures. Elected as a Fellow of the American Folklore Society in 2005, Dorry is the author of *Fire in the Plaça: Catalan Festival Politics after Franco* (2003), *Humble Theory: Folklore's Grasp on Social Life* (2016), and *Sustaining Interdisciplinary Collaboration: A Guide for the Academy* (with Regina Bendix and Kilian Bizer, 2017). Dorry served as the Director of the Center for Folklore Studies from 2005 until 2014, and she is currently President-Elect of the American Folklore Society.

EIGHTEENTH-CENTURY

We made three appointments in this field, Sandra Macpherson in 1996, and David Brewer and Roxann Wheeler, both in 1999. Sandra was recruited away by the University of Chicago in 1999, but, after earning tenure there, she returned to the Department in 2009 so that she and her partner, Luke Wilson, could stop commuting. In addition to her stellar work in eighteenth-century studies, Sandra is a core member of the group in critical theory. She is the author of *Harm's Way: Tragic Responsibility and the Novel Form* (2010).

David Brewer has expertise not only in the eighteenth-century but also in book history. He is the author of *The Afterlife of Character, 1726–1825* (2005), and editor of Richard Brinsley Sheridan, *The Rivals,* and George Colman the Elder, *Polly Honeycombe* (2012). At the time of writing, David has two collaborative books forthcoming, *The Book in Britain: A Historical Introduction,* and *Interacting with Print: Elements of Reading in the Era of Print Saturation.*

Roxann Wheeler, who is also an expert in feminist theory, is the author of *The Complexion of Race: Categories of Difference in Eighteenth-Century British Culture* (2000) and is currently associate editor of *Studies in Eighteenth-Century Culture.*

VICTORIAN

In 2001, we hired Aman Garcha. Aman is the author of *From Sketch to Novel: The Development of Victorian Fiction* (2009) and numerous essays on Victorian subjects and the profession. He has three times been chosen by the

FIGURE 9.3. Dorothy Noyes

graduate students as Graduate Professor of the Year, and he is currently in the midst of setting a Departmental record—one that I suspect will never be broken—for longest term as Director of Graduate Studies. He is now in year five.

LINGUISTICS

In 2002 we added Galey Modan. A specialist in sociolinguistics, Galey is the author of *Turf Wars: Discourse, Diversity, and the Politics of Place* (2007) and numerous essays on matters ranging from the role of language in multiethnic urban formations to discourses surrounding end-of-life situations.

THE DEPARTMENTAL TEACHING EXCELLENCE AWARD

In one of its periodic turns to the importance of teaching at OSU, the central administration opened a three-year window (1998–2000) in which it offered an award for outstanding teaching by Departments, an award designed to recognize teaching at all levels by all members of the teaching staff. The administration showed it was serious about the award by attaching a prize of $25,000 to a Department's base budget. It would be a reward that keeps on rewarding. Since English has consistently valued teaching, we applied and succeeded in the second year, thanks primarily to the work of our teachers from basic writing to the graduate seminar classrooms. But we also succeeded because of the outstanding proposal prepared by Sebastian Knowles, who proudly trumpeted our widespread pedagogical achievements. He captured the enthusiastic attitude of our teaching staff by substituting "English" for first noun in Samuel Johnson's famous line that "To be tired of London is to be tired of life."

How we have used the money is another sign of the Department's gradual evolution toward the federation model. We chose to use the bulk of the 25K to enhance the graduate program by adding the workshop component to it, a feature that continues to this day. Here's the current description from the Department website.

> The Graduate Workshops provide opportunities to enrich the department's formal graduate curriculum by regularly bringing in scholars from other institutions to discuss their recently published and current work with students and faculty. Typically, the department is able to offer 3 to 5 Workshops per academic year, which rotate among fields. Each Workshop is organized by a faculty coordinator, and students enroll by signing up with the graduate studies office.
>
> The visiting speaker participates in two events: a public lecture or other kind of formal presentation, open to all members of the department and university community, and a closed session with graduate students who have enrolled in the Workshop. For the smaller Workshop, the visiting speaker assigns a text or group of texts for discussion (his or her own work or some other work relevant to the speaker's current interests). Students read the assigned texts on their own and submit short position papers to the faculty coordinator. The completion of these short essays, in combination with student participation, determine whether a student receives a grade of "S" (Satisfactory) or "U" (Unsatisfactory) for the Workshop.

PROJECT NARRATIVE

I close this chapter with an account of the formation and evolution of Project Narrative, both because it had its origins in Selective Investment and because it further illustrates how the omnibus morphed into a federation.

In the Autumn of 2005, the University launched another initiative to enhance its reputation, a follow-up to Selective Investment called Targeted Investment in Excellence (TIE). It, too, was designed to improve both the quality and the rankings of OSU, but, where SI provided funds for senior hiring, TIE provided funds for research programs conceived and executed by current OSU faculty. In special cases, however, TIE funds could be used to hire new faculty. Awards would be for $500,000, disbursed over the next five years. Departments were invited to submit proposals to Colleges, and then Deans would rank those proposals and send them on to the Provost, who, in consultation with a faculty committee, would make the final decisions. The call also stipulated that any dean who advanced a proposal to the Provost would have to agree to find College funds to support the project if the Provost did not choose it.

When the call for TIE proposals came out in the Autumn of 2005, Brian, David, Frederick and I collaborated on the proposal for Project Narrative. Recognizing that the definition of "narrative" was itself a contested issue in the field, we opted for a broad understanding of the term ("the representation of a linked sequence of events") that would include traditional literary narratives (novel, short story, lifewriting), history, film, television, graphic narrative, digital narrative, and more. We described Project Narrative's mission as promoting "cutting-edge research and teaching on narrative and narrative theory," and we laid out a plan for symposia, lecture series, and collaborations with other groups in the international narrative theory community. We also highlighted publications that would follow from these activities.

Fortunately, our proposal met with favor at both the Department and College levels. Furthermore, much to our delight, Dean of Humanities John Roberts and his committee recommended that we revise the budget to include a provision for a new hire. The Provost did not select Project Narrative, but, consistent with TIE's rules of engagement, the College provided its funding for the first five years, 2006–11.

During the 2007–08 academic year, we conducted the search for the additional faculty member, with Chair Valerie Lee ably directing the process and David Herman serving as committee chair. We were delighted to be able to recruit Robyn Warhol from the University of Vermont, and she joined the Department and Project Narrative in 2009.

In its first five years (2006–11) Project Narrative focused on carrying out the plans in its proposal, highlights of which included three symposia, one on Narrative Theory and Multiethnic Narratives (coordinated by Frederick Aldama), one on Narrative, Science, and Performance (coordinated by me), and the other on Queer and Feminist Narratologies (coordinated by Robyn

FIGURE 9.4. Robyn Warhol

Warhol). Each symposium led to a significant publication: *Analyzing World Fiction,* edited by Aldama, a special issue of *Narrative* devoted to Narrative, Science, and Performance (edited by me), and *Narrative Theory Unbound,* co-edited by Robyn Warhol and Susan S. Lanser of Brandeis University. During this period, David Herman, Brian McHale, and I also co-edited *Teaching Narrative Theory,* which appeared in 2010 in the MLA series on Approaches to Teaching, and included essays by each of us and by Frederick and Robyn as well.

Robyn's hiring expanded the core group of Project Narrative faculty to five, and that group has continued to grow. Over the last several years, Angus Fletcher, Jared Gardner, Sean O'Sullivan, Amy Shuman (all from English), Julia Watson (from Comparative Studies), and Katra Byram (from German) have brought their energy and expertise to our enterprise. These new members have made it easier for PN to absorb the loss of David Herman, who in 2013 took a position as Professor of Engaged Humanities at Durham University in England. Project Narrative now has expertise in cognitive, rhetorical, feminist, queer, and other approaches to narrative as well as in print, graphic, film, and television narrative.

In this respect, Project Narrative reflects the breadth and diversity of the larger international narrative studies community, which has itself become increasingly diverse and interdisciplinary over the last twenty-five years. Indeed, it is not possible to summarize the diversity of the field in a short space, but I can highlight three significant and often overlapping movements that our group has both contributed to and been influenced by. The first is the Narrative Turn, the recognition that storytelling is a phenomenon central not just to literary studies but to multiple other disciplines, especially law, medicine, and business. At Ohio State, faculty in Project Narrative have been instrumental in the development of a new interdisciplinary undergraduate minor in the Medical Humanities and of an interdisciplinary M.A. in the Medical Humanities and Social Sciences. The second movement is the flourishing interest in Narrative across Media, the recognition that the affordances of different media enable storytellers to do significantly different things with the elements of narrative and that narrative theory needs to account for these differences. The third movement is interest in the efficacy of narrative—the multiple ways in which storytelling, fictional or nonfictional, has real world consequences. To take just one example, faculty in Project Narrative have collaborated with scholars in the Medical School and in Biological Sciences working on treatments for Infectious Diseases to help create more effective stories about their research and what it means for dealing with the growing problem of antimicrobial resistance (a.k.a. the problem of "superbugs").

During our first five years, we established two ongoing programs that directly connect Project Narrative to the larger international network of narrative studies. (1) Every year we host Visiting Scholars for periods ranging from several weeks to two semesters. These scholars have come from the US, Canada, England, Belgium, Germany, Italy, Denmark, Norway, South Africa, China, Australia, and elsewhere. The Visiting Scholars sit in on classes, work on their projects, interact with our graduate students, and do presentations of their work. (2) Since 2010, we have run the Project Narrative Summer Institute, a two-week workshop for scholars who want to learn more about narrative theory. Every year we designate a particular theme, alternating between general ones (e.g., "Narrative Theory: Foundations and Innovations") and more specific ones (e.g., "Narrative Theory and Visual Narrative"; "Queer and Feminist Narrative Theory"), and we attract 16–24 participants—again from around the world.

In 2002, Valerie Lee succeeded me as Chair. Reading Valerie's contributions to this history will give you some sense of how remarkable she is, and how fortunate the Department was to have her at the helm until 2009.

EPILOGUE

Into the Twenty-First Century

WE HAVE CHOSEN, for various reasons, to keep our history of the English Department historical: not to bring it up to the present. So we can't, for example, give an account of the many important and even extraordinary faculty appointments within the recent past. But for the record we should provide a bare sense of the pattern of the Department's leadership.

Certainly, the new governance in the new century was "historical" in key ways. Even beyond her many major accomplishments as a leader, Valerie Lee's appointment as Chair of the Department of English was clearly significant and notable. Lee was the first woman, and the first African American, to assume that role, which she fulfilled from 2002 until 2009. For an all-too brief account of her career and many accomplishments, see Chapter 8, where we have provided a sense of her accomplishments in research and scholarship (as in *Granny Midwives and Black Women Writers: Double-Dutched Readings* and *The Prentice Hall Anthology of African American Women's Literature*), teaching (as evidenced by her University Alumni Award for Distinguished Teaching), and service (her University Faculty Award for Distinguished University Service), and her numerous roles within University administration (as Chair not only of the English Department, but also of Women's, Gender, and Sexuality Studies and African American and African Studies, as well as Vice President for Outreach and Engagement, the Vice Provost for Diversity and Inclusion, and the chief Diversity Officer for the University.

FIGURE 10.1. Valerie Lee

In another first, Richard Dutton then became the first English person to chair English. A Renaissance scholar, he had come from the University of Lancaster in 2003. He is the author of *Mastering the Revels: The Regulation and Censorship of English Renaissance Drama* (1991), *Licensing, Censorship and Authorship in Early Modern England* (2000), and of several books on Ben Jonson and William Shakespeare, including *William Shakespeare: A Literary Life* (1989), part of the *Literary Lives* series of which he is the general editor. He served as Chair until 2013 and retired in 2015.

Sebastian Knowles—on whose career, see Chapter 8—was Chair for a brief time, 2013–14. After Steven Fink served a short term as Acting Chair, Richard Dutton was Interim Chair until Debra Moddelmog became Chair in the fall of 2014. For her career, also see Chapter 8. Moddelmog left Ohio State in 2016, to become Dean of the College of Liberal Arts at the University of Nevada, Reno.

The new Chair was—and is, as of this writing—Robyn Warhol, who came to the Department and Project Narrative from the University of Vermont. Warhol is the author of, among other works, *Gendered Interventions: Narrative Discourse in the Victorian Novel* (1989) and *Having a Good Cry: Effeminate Feelings and Popular Forms* (2003). With Helena Michie, she co-authored *Love*

FIGURE 10.2. Richard Dutton

among the Archives: Writing the Lives of George Scharf, Victorian Bachelor, which won the North American Victorian Studies Association's Best Book of the Year for 2015. For other aspects of Warhol's career, see the accounts by Jim Phelan of Project Narrative in Chapter 7 and by Valerie Lee of Women's and Gender Studies in Chapter 8.

Behind our entire project of this history of the Department is a conviction that knowing something of what we in the Department have done is important as we move into the future. Our sense of our tradition as well as of our continuing mission *matters*. Whatever we aver about the birth and future of the cosmos, the universe will expand—or not. Whatever we may think about the "theory" of evolution, the world and its inhabitants will evolve. We may claim that the sun revolves around the earth or the earth around the sun; in any case, the planets will do their thing. Whether we believe in luck is irrelevant to the results of a throw of our dice. But human beings and what they do are not so free of—so cut off from—what they say or believe or know about themselves and their history.

FIGURE 10.3. The Chairs, as of the Lee Years: John Gabel, James Phelan, Julian Markels, Valerie Lee, Al Kuhn, Morris Beja

We hope we have shown how much the Department has grown and changed over the years—and how much of its rich history it has retained and preserved, as well. The English Department of today is not your grandparent's or great-grandparent's English Department. But it sort of is, too.

We have tried to be faithful to the Department's past, always remembering that it's not even past.

ACKNOWLEDGMENTS

WE HAVE so many people to thank that our fear is that we'll somehow not include everyone.

Let us mention, first, some of our sources. Many of course are listed in our "Works Cited," but others must be singled out. A key person in this respect is Nancy Dasher, whose mimeographed history of the Department for the University's centenary in 1970 was, from the start, an invaluable guide. We learned from all those who contributed to Charles Wheeler's project, *The Estrich Years, 1952–1964: Personal Reminiscences* (including Richard D. Altick, W. Todd Furniss, Julian Markels, Frances Ebstein Shapiro, Eric Solomon, and Andrew Wright), and none more than from Charles himself, whose contribution is not only about Bob Estrich but also about other notable figures of his time. We also owe a debt to Charles's typescript, "The O. S. U. Campus Disorders of 1970: A Personal View." Another typescript we drew upon is Al Kuhn's "Words in Time: Essays and Occasions."

Among published works by colleagues we have to mention as especially valuable are Frank Donoghue's *The Last Professors: The Corporate University and the Fate of the Humanities*; Julian Markels's *From Buchenwald to Havana: The Life and Opinions of a Socialist Professor*; James Phelan's *Beyond the Tenure Track: Fifteen Months in the Life of an English Professor*; and Elizabeth Renker's *The Origins of American Literature Studies: An Institutional History*.

Other very helpful sources have included Claire Cooper, for information about Gertrude Lucille Robinson; Betty Gabel, for answering questions, for providing information we never thought to ask about, and for terrific stories and vivid impressions about John Gabel and other friends and colleagues; Michelle Drobik and Kevlin C. Haire of University Archives for help with both photographs and documents.

The staff of the Department of English—notably Wayne Lovely and Tracee Mohler—were invariably helpful and responsive to our requests (and problems).

We're particularly indebted to all current or retired faculty, and to former students, who responded to our queries—and to our pestering requests for photographs.

Readers of this book obviously realize our tremendous debts to a number of colleagues who actually wrote important sections for us. We must mention them here: David Frantz and Julian Markels, "Sports in the Department of English"; John Hellmann, "History of the Regional Campuses"; Michelle Herman, "Creative Writing"; Valerie Lee, "African American Literature in Ohio State's Department of English" and "Women's and Gender Studies"; Andrea Abernethy Lunsford, "Rhetoric and Composition"; Linda Mizejewski, "Film Studies in the English Department"; Patrick Mullen and Amy Shuman, "Folklore"; James Phelan, "Critical Theory" and the entirety of Chapter 9.

We benefited from material as well as moral support from a number of colleagues: David Frantz, Andrea Lunsford, Debra Moddelmog, Beverly Moss, Robyn Warhol, and Peter Hahn and Stephen Petrill of the Division of Arts and Humanities.

Early on, we were fortunate to have Andrew Smart as a Graduate Associate. Andrew marvelously got into the spirit of the whole project, which tied in with his own interests in academic history.

Eleni R. Beja provided invaluable and absolutely and embarrassingly necessary help with images and photographs to a couple of fellas with limited (minimal) technical expertise.

Three people read entire drafts of this manuscript, providing wonderful editorial advice and counsel: David Frantz, Ellen Carol Jones, and Andrea Lunsford.

Finally, and as always, we're humbly grateful for immeasurable support of innumerable kinds to Ellen Carol Jones and Kay Bea Jones. Only they know how much we owe them, and we hope they do.

IN MEMORIAM

Christian Zacher, 1941–2019

Chris saw this history to its completion, and through special efforts by The Ohio State University Press was presented with the proofs to the book just days before he died.

WORKS CITED

The list below is of sources specifically cited or quoted within our text. It does not, for example, include the titles of faculty publications that are mentioned in passing.

Annual Reports of the Board of Trustees. See http://kb.osu.edu/dspace/handle/1811/53827/browse?order=DESC&rpp=20&sort_by=2&etal=-1&offset=100&type=dateissued.

Beja, Morris, David Frantz, Mary Jo Hlay, James Kincaid, Melanie Lusk, and Julian Markels. "Report of the Self-Study Committee of the English Department, The Ohio State University," 1978. Typescript. Department of English files.

Committee of Inquiry. "The Spring Events at Ohio State: A Report of the Committee of Inquiry to the Faculty Council," November 10, 1970. Typescript. Department of English files.

Connors, Robert J. "Edward P. J. Corbett: Memoriam." *Rhetoric Review* 17.1 (1998): 126–131.

Course Offerings Bulletin of the College of Arts, Philosophy and Science, 1905. See ARV_UREG_College_Of_Arts_Philosophy_And_Science_1905-1906.pdf.

Crowley, Sharon. *Composition in the University: Historical and Polemical Essays.* University of Pittsburgh P., 1997.

Dasher, Nancy. *"Of What Is Past, or Passing . . .": A Brief History of the Department of English, The Ohio State University.* The Ohio State University Centennial Histories, College of Humanities, 1970.

"Department Staff List from 1911 to 2000.exlsx," https://osu.app.box.com/files/0/f/4178714451/1/f_32190112867.

Donoghue, Frank J. *The Last Professors: The Corporate University and the Fate of the Humanities.* Fordham University P., 2008.

Editorial, *Columbus Evening Dispatch* (June 21, 1935): 4-A.

Ferguson, Suzanne. "Autumn Graduate Registration in English," memo of Fall Quarter 1979.

Fitch, Noel Riley. *Sylvia Beach and the Lost Generation: A History of Literary Paris in the Twenties and Thirties.* W. W. Norton, 1983.

Goerler, Raimund E. *The Ohio State University: An Illustrated History.* Ohio State University P., 2011.

Haverstock, Mary Sayre. *George Bellows: An Artist in Action.* Merrell / Columbus Museum of Art, 2007.

Holmes, Charles S. *The Clocks of Columbus: The Literary Career of James Thurber.* Atheneum, 1972.

Kuhn, Albert J. "Words in Time: Essays and Occasions," 2006. Typescript.

Laney, Joni, and Mary Ruth Laney Reilly, "Family Reflections on Ruth W. Hughey, 1899–1980," in "Emory Women Writers Research Project," http://womenwriters.library.emory.edu/content.php?level=div&id=hughey_800&document=hughey.

"Largest Faculty Meeting in History." *Ohio State University Monthly* (June 1962): 12–28.

Markels, Julian. *From Buchenwald to Havana: The Life and Opinions of a Socialist Professor.* Evening Street P., 2012.

Mendenhall, Annie S. "Joseph V. Denney, the Land-Grant Mission, and Rhetorical Education at Ohio State: An Institutional History." *College English* 74 (November 2011): 131–156.

Mendenhall, T. C. *The First Faculty . . . An Address Given on The Occasion of the Semicentennial Celebration of the Ohio State University, October 15, 1920.* Columbus? 1920?

MLA Handbook: Eighth Edition. Modern Language Association of America, 2016.

Newdick, Robert S. *Newdick's Season of Frost: An Interrupted Biography of Robert Frost.* Edited by William A. Sutton. State University of New York P., 1976.

Phelan, James. *Beyond the Tenure Track: Fifteen Months in the Life of an English Professor.* Ohio State University P., 1991.

Pollard, James E. *History of the Ohio State University: The Story of Its First Seventy-Five Years, 1873–1948.* Ohio State University P., 1952.

Record of Proceedings of the Board of Trustees of The Ohio State University from June 30, 1900, to July 1, 1904.

Renker, Elizabeth. *The Origins of American Literature Studies: An Institutional History.* Cambridge University P., 2007.

Richards, I. A. *The Philosophy of Rhetoric.* New York: Oxford University P., 1936.

Shkurti, William J. *The Ohio State University in the Sixties: The Unraveling of the Old Order.* Ohio State University P., 2016.

Solomon, Eric. "Free Speech at Ohio State." *The Troubled Campus,* edited by the Editors of the *Atlantic,* Little Brown and Co., 1966, pp. 63–76.

Steward, Samuel M. *Chapters from an Autobiography.* Grey Fox P., 1981.

Steward, Samuel M., ed. *Dear Sammy: Letters from Gertrude Stein and Alice B. Toklas.* Houghton Mifflin, 1977.

Thurber, James. *The Thurber Album.* Simon and Schuster, 1952.

Thurber, James. "He Cast a Light: Of Learning, of Scholarship, of Laughter, of Wisdom," *Ohio State Monthly* (May 1960): 6–7. Speech at dedication of Denney Hall, April 1, 1960.

Thurber, James, and Elliott Nugent. *The Male Animal.* (In Burns Mantle, ed., *The Best Plays of 1939–40 and the Year Book of the Drama in America.* Dodd, Mead and Co., 1940, pp. 215–249.)

Wheeler, Charles, ed. *The Estrich Years, 1952–1964: Personal Reminiscences.* Department of English, 1996. Pamphlet. Contains reminiscences by Richard D. Altick, Morris Beja, W.

Todd Furniss, Julian Markels, Frances Ebstein Shapiro, Eric Solomon, Charles Wheeler, and Andrew Wright.

Wheeler, Charles. "The O. S. U. Campus Disorders of 1970: A Personal View." Undated typescript, with unnumbered pages. Also available at https://library.osu.edu/projects/dissent-eyewitness/images/wheeler_reaction.pdf.

Woodson, Thomas. "The Center for Textual Studies and the Centenary Edition of the Works of Nathaniel Hawthorne." *Impromptu: A Newsletter* (Department of English) 2.2 (Spring 1985): 4.

Zacher, Christian, and Paul E. Szarmach. "In Memoriam: Stanley J. Kahrl (1931–89)." *Old English Newsletter* 23.1 (1989): 15.

INDEX

Mitchel, Koritha, 154

Mitchell, Rand, 123

Mitchell, W. J. Thomas, 81–82, 84, 116

Mizejewski, Linda, 139, 161–63, 171

Modan, Galey, 183

Moddelmog, Debra, 33, 134, 134 fig. 8.5, 137, 139, 190

Modern Language Association, 9, 29, 74, 132

Modernism, 128

Moore, Alyce, 41, 64, 87

Morrison, Toni, 120, 135, 151, 159

Moss, Beverly, 37n23, 76, 84, 132, 146, 146 fig. 8.8, 152, 155

Mountford, Roxanne, 79

Mowoe, Isaac, 70

Mozart, Wolfgang Amadeus, 119

Mukherjee, Bharati, 135

Mulderig, Gerald, 78

Mullen, Patrick, 23, 85–86, 96–101, 119, 122, 158, 160n19

Munday, Mildred Brand, 81, 92, 135, 140

Murray, Rolland, 152

Murray, Thomas, 144

Muste, A. J., 46

Muste, Jean, 46

Muste, John M., 46, 47 fig. 4.5, 84, 87, 90, 90n14

Myers, Robert Mason, 135

Nakadate, Neil, 147

Nancy Dasher Award, 31, 147

Nathaniel Hawthorne Society, 55

National Book Award, 176

National Council of Teachers of English, 73–74, 119

National Endowment for the Humanities, 23, 144, 147, 152

National Guard, 90–93, 93 fig. 5.10, 136, 157

National Women's Studies Association, 137–38

Nelms, Jerry, 79

Nemzer, Louis, 93

New Chaucer Society, 24, 175

New York University, 417–18

Newark campus, 55

Newdick, Robert S., 19

Newlyn, Andrea, 137

Newton, Pauline, 34

Nicolas, Melissa, 146

Nin, Anaïs, 142

Nixon, Richard M., 77, 92

Norman, John, 181

Noyes, Dorothy, 99, 182, 183 fig. 9.3

Nugent, Elliott, 12–13

O'Brien O'Keeffe, Katherine, 153n11

Odlin, Terrence, 76, 129–30

Oforlea, Aaron, 160

O'Hare, Frank, 76, 114, 119, 168 fig. 8.13

Ohio Agricultural and Mechanical College, 1

Ohio Humanities Council, 131

Ohio Impromptu, 123

Ohio State University Press, The, 26, 29, 115, 166, 175

Ohioana Award, 176

O'Neill, William, 112

Oregon State, 78

Ornstein, Robert, 112

Orwell, George, 50n8, 118

O'Sullivan, Sean, 163, 186

Overmeyer, Janet, 68

Papper, Carole, 79, 132, 146

Parker, William Riley, 25

Parks, Steve, 146

Passe, Martha E., 30

Pearce, Roy Harvey, 27–29, 31, 42

Pennsylvania State University, 79

Percival, Milton O., 19, 21–22, 34

Phelan, Jim, 85–86, 105, 115, 115 fig. 7.2, 116–19, 143, 155, 166, 168 fig. 8.13, 169–71, 192 fig. 10.3

Phi Beta Kappa, 54

Philosophy Department, 31, 117

Photography and Cinema Department, 161

Piontek, Thomas, 137, 162, 168 fig. 8.13

Pipes, Candice, 160

CPSIA information can be obtained
at www.ICGtesting.com
Printed in the USA
LVHW091047030220
645656LV00001B/1

9 781733 534000